FIVE GOOD
MINUTES
at work

100 Mindful Practices to
Help You Relieve Stress and
Bring Your Best to Work

Jeffrey Brantley, M.D.

Wendy Millstine

MJF BOOKS   NEW YORK

Published by MJF Books
Fine Communications
322 Eighth Avenue
New York, NY 10001

Five Good Minutes at Work
LC Control Number: 2013955635
ISBN 978-1-60671-240-5

This edition is published by MJF Books in arrangement
with New Harbinger Publications, Inc.

This publication is designed to provide accurate and authoritative
information in regard to the subject matter covered. It is sold with the
understanding that the publishers are not engaged in rendering psychological,
financial, legal, or other professional services. If expert assistance or counseling
is needed, the services of a competent professional should be sought.

DESIGNED BY LISA CHOVNICK

Printed in the United States of America.

MJF Books and the MJF colophon are trademarks of Fine Creative Media, Inc.

QF   10   9   8   7   6   5   4   3   2   1

THIS BOOK IS DEDICATED TO EVERYONE WHO WORKS.
MAY YOU FIND GREATER HAPPINESS AND A RICHER LIFE
THROUGH YOUR EFFORTS. MAY THE ENTIRE WORLD
BENEFIT FROM YOUR GIFTS.

—JB

FOR JUDY AND MATTHEW MCKAY, WHOSE
UNCEASING BELIEF, SUPPORT, AND KINDNESS HAVE
GUIDED ME ON THIS REWARDING JOURNEY AND WHO
HAVE HELPED SHINE A MINDFUL LIGHT INTO
EVERY CORNER OF MY LIFE.

—WM

Contents

CONTENTS

DOING YOUR WORK MORE EFFECTIVELY 39

CONTENTS

CONTENTS

CONTENTS

Introduction

Is it possible that work—perhaps even *your* work—in whatever shape or location it occurs, could somehow nurture a deeper sense of connection with others and a greater sense of awe and appreciation for the mystery of being alive?

Could your working life be more satisfying?

Would you like to work more effectively? Would you like to function with more ease and less stress? Would you like to develop more enjoyable relationships with those you work with?

How might any of these things happen?

In our previous two books, *Five Good Minutes: 100 Morning Practices to Help You Stay Calm and Focused All Day Long* and *Five Good Minutes in the Evening: 100 Mindful Practices to Help You Unwind from the Day and Make the Most of Your Night*, we suggested that even the busiest person can take "five good minutes" to do a deliberate practice that can help shift their experience of life in a significant and even profound way.

The five-good-minutes concept is simple: take the time, for just five minutes (of course you can do longer!) to be present mindfully, to set a clear intention for yourself, and to act wholeheartedly, without attachment to any outcome, as you explore a focused practice or activity.

By practicing, in a friendly and curious way, the skills of mindful presence, clear intention, and wholehearted action, you open the possibility that exciting and enriching new experiences might arise in one of the most familiar places of your life—your work or professional world!

The 100 practices in this book are all focused on life as it happens while you work. They offer the possibility of recovering your heart and soul through the working life, as well as enriching the experiences of mind and body, all while performing with increasing effectiveness.

The practices are designed to be easy and practical—specific and concrete—also inviting and fun. You can do any of them right away, on the job. Some are more lighthearted, while others invite a more reflective experience. You may even find some to be uplifting and inspiring, offering a new vision of your working life (and your larger journey through life) that perhaps you had not appreciated before.

MEETING YOUR LIFE, HERE, IN THE PRESENT MOMENT

The foundation of your five good minutes is learning to establish presence through *mindfulness*. Mindfulness happens as you pay attention (to your breath, your body, or just about anything that is happening in or around you) on purpose, in a friendly and nonjudging way.

Life, whether you are working, playing, or resting, happens only in the present moment. The skills of mindfulness that you will develop through the practices in this book can help you inhabit the present moment (and thus your life) more consciously and joyfully.

In the "Foundation" section of this book, you will find clear and easy-to-follow instructions for developing your skills at being mindful. Feel free to refer back to these instructions whenever you need to as you explore the various practices. As you gain more and more experience with the practices, you will discover the naturalness and ease of being present, for example, simply by breathing mindfully, listening mindfully to sounds, or attending mindfully to the sensations of your body.

DON'T BELIEVE EVERYTHING
YOU THINK

Done mindfully and wholeheartedly, each of the 100 practices in this book offers you the possibility of experiencing some familiar aspect of your daily life at work in a different way. These fresh ways of experiencing yourself and your working life can provide you with insight and new understandings, increase ease, reduce stress, and even make how you approach your work healthier and safer.

It is all too easy to become distracted as we work.

Easy to fall into old habits of inattention and distraction. Easy to make up stories that aren't true.

Easy to be hijacked by unpleasant feelings like worry, anger, or even physical discomfort or pain.

Easy to be pulled out of ourselves and out of the present moment by the momentum of busyness or the feeling of being disconnected and isolated.

In such times of worry and hurry, of isolation and distraction, one's ability to work effectively suffers, as does the ability to work in an emotionally intelligent way. And, beset by such distractions, one may even work in ways that are physically harmful or dangerous.

This book, like our previous two, is dedicated to helping you become the best person you can be and to assist you in opening to the most rewarding life you can have.

And there is a larger perspective.

As authors, we believe that as each individual finds more joy and ease and more peace and understanding in their own life, many others benefit as well.

In that sense of interconnectedness, we invite you to consider the possibility that there could be benefits far beyond your immediate experience whenever you do even one of these practices. Discovering something new about your interrelatedness to others can be an additional benefit arising from your practice.

But you don't need to worry about that now; just try some practices and see for yourself. And remember, what you think you know before doing a practice might not be so true afterward! You are encouraged to be open to hidden surprises in the practices.

The focus in this book is explicitly on your working life and ways to operate and live there while being as present and connected, and as happy and healthy, as possible.

You will find the practices in this book grouped into four major sections, each focusing on a particular aspect of working life. The sections are:

- *doing your work more effectively*

- *reducing stress at work*

- *working more intelligently & compassionately with others*

- *travel, deadlines, frustrations, & other opportunities*

Each section contains practices and exercises you can do in just five minutes, based on being present, setting your intention, and acting wholeheartedly. Each practice has the power to shift your perspective and to invoke change in your life.

So, this book is for you, or perhaps someone you love who works, if you think that:

- *working more effectively and efficiently is important*

- *enjoying more ease and reducing stress at work sounds appealing*

- *relationships with people at work could be more joyful and kinder*

- *everyday frustrations, deadlines, and upsets could be handled better*

- *a richer appreciation of life's awe and mystery might be found in the activities of daily work*

We have great confidence in the power of these practices and in your ability to enrich your life through presence, intention, and wholehearted action.

Now, all that remains is for you to dive in—discover what is possible—and enjoy!

PART ONE

THE
FOUNDATION

WHAT IS YOUR RELATIONSHIP
TO YOUR WORK (AND LIFE)?

What is work life like for you? Today? Right now?

Would you like more happiness and success in your job? Would you like to feel more interested and excited there?

Are you interested in the possibility that your work could be a passageway to a different view of yourself and others and a fresh way of approaching life? This view, or understanding, includes curiosity and appreciation for the mysterious and awe inspiring and attention to heart and soul, as well as mind and body.

By "heart" we mean a greater openness and sense of connection to others and to experience.

By "soul" we mean a deeper appreciation for and understanding of something greater than our ego-centered ways of living.

The key to enriching your work experience and to making new and intriguing discoveries within it lies very likely in paying attention to three dimensions of your experience as you work.

These are the dimensions: *how you are relating to yourself*—psychologically, emotionally, and physically; *how you are relating to those around you*—what stories do you tell yourself about you and them and your relationships with them; and *how you are relating to the actual work you are doing*—what stories do you tell yourself about the work, its value, and the quality you create?

WHOM THIS BOOK IS FOR

This book is for *anyone* who works at *any* job, including nonpaid work and volunteers. It is for anyone who wants more—satisfaction, joy, peace, effectiveness, or reward—from that work.

This book and the practices it contains are intended to be enjoyable, challenging, supportive, and to contain the possibility of powerful transformation.

But to gain maximum benefit from the practices offered here, you will have to do some work. You will need some resolve, a bit of curiosity, and the willingness to try something new and different. Most of all, you will be invited to consider and to explore the possibility that you are more than you may have realized: more alive, more kind and generous, more brave and steadfast, even more powerful and effective than you may have imagined.

This is a book that depends upon *learning by doing*. The 100 different practices are to be experienced, not just read. It is in those experiences that you will find all the benefits that are possible. By actually doing (not just reading about) the practices based on skills of being present, setting intention, and acting wholeheartedly, you will open the doorway to possibilities and understandings about yourself and work that exist now only as potentials.

The practices in this book are easier than you might think, and what's more, they are fun and interesting!

All you need is some curiosity and the willingness to "try on" any of the practices that call to you. Take them seriously enough to "work" them, perhaps several times. Then, see if you experience any effects following from your practice. See for yourself. Do only the ones that actually make a positive difference for you.

This is a *practical* book. It offers you specific activities and tools crafted for use on the job. The practices hold the possibility of changing how you experience, perceive, and cope with everything, from what you do to how you do it to whom you do it with. You will find new choices and more responses available, and your relationship to yourself and your life, especially your work life, can change in very interesting and even unexpected ways.

However, this book is *not* a magic potion. It probably won't get you a pay raise (at least not immediately), and you shouldn't count on it to change someone else's behavior. It will not put new paint on your walls or dim that loud noise outside or change any one of countless other conditions now present.

What *can* happen, if you start to work with these practices, is that you can begin to change. You could find yourself becoming more relaxed, more attentive, more receptive, more curious, more lighthearted, less critical, less anxious, or less driven. As that happens, who knows what other things may change?

WHAT ARE "FIVE GOOD MINUTES"?

The five-good-minutes concept is simple. Take a minute to establish mindfulness, take some time to set a clear intention, and then spend your remaining time doing a focused activity wholeheartedly from your conscious base in the present moment.

Five Good Minutes
Being present, setting intention, acting wholeheartedly.

Doing your five good minutes means deliberately stopping and stepping out of the momentum and habitual energy (the familiar and often unconscious ways of thinking, feeling, and inhabiting your body) pushing you through this moment of your life. It means paying attention, waking up a bit more, and directing attention and activity in a fresh way.

The wholehearted activity you undertake can be literally anything. The practices here focus on work situations, on managing stress, on relationships, and even on special situations like travel or deadlines.

HOW MIGHT FIVE GOOD MINUTES HELP YOU?

Being present is about paying attention and being more mindful. Mindfulness is about nonjudging and kind awareness. Intention and wholeheartedness are about focus and engagement.

Besides holding the potential for enriching heart and soul, practicing the art and skills of mindfulness, intention, and engagement can have a significant impact in some very practical ways toward working more safely, working smarter, and working with greater interest and enthusiasm.

Working More Safely

When people work without mindfulness, without proper attention focused on the present moment, they are at greater risk for hurting themselves.

This risk for injury exists, of course, in "risky" activities— heavy lifting, awkward movements, and improper methods of physical exertion, as well as in dangerous environments or when handling toxic materials.

What often goes unrecognized—even in jobs that seem relatively safe—are conditions of excessive repetitive movements, working too long without a break, and general inattention to the signals of body and mind that rest and relaxation are needed.

Finally (and perhaps most importantly), increased risk

of injury seems related to a lack of self-awareness about feelings, thoughts, and your inner life. It can be said that it isn't the stress but how you handle it that counts. By learning to attend to and manage your levels of stress while knowing what feelings and thoughts are present, coloring your experience and behavior in the present moment, you will empower yourself to work from a foundation of maximum safety.

In this book, you will find practices intended to sharpen your attention skills, help you relax mind and body, and tune in more easily to the events of your inner and outer experience throughout the workday. Being more attentive, present, and more at ease as you work can help you support health and safety throughout your day.

Working with Emotional Intelligence

In his best-selling books *Emotional Intelligence* (1995) and *Working with Emotional Intelligence* (1998), author Daniel Goleman points out how the most effective people in many walks of life express intelligence in a different way.

What Goleman means by this is that truly effective people are skillful about recognizing and managing their emotions, getting along with others, and working in teams. He reports a tremendous positive response to his work from the business community.

Building on earlier research, Goleman identifies five domains of emotional intelligence: *self-awareness, managing one's own emotions, capacity to motivate oneself, ability to recognize accurately others' emotions*, and *ability to handle relationships skillfully*.

Because of the common practices of 24/7 accountability, seventy- and eighty-hour workweeks, rapid technical innovations, increased rates of change, global competition, and waves of organizational downsizing, learning to work in an emotionally intelligent way is now more crucial than ever.

You will find practices in this book that help you grow more aware of your inner life, including feelings and thoughts. You will find practices to help you make space for upset, cope more effectively, and bring more friendly attention to your experience as it unfolds. And there are practices to help you hear others more accurately, respond to them more thoughtfully, and relate to them more skillfully.

Working with More Joy and Less Stress

Could attention to your inner life and learning to direct attention and awareness explicitly have a positive impact on your sense of joy and ease? Could such skills of attention and presence—of mindfulness—be beneficial in any external situation, including one's work site? Could regular practice of meditation as an attention and awareness activity affect the physical function of brain and body? There is some evidence to suggest that the answer to these questions is "yes."

Mindfulness-based stress reduction (MBSR) is the name of an approach to managing stress and promoting health that is now about twenty-five years old. MBSR was started by Jon Kabat-Zinn and his colleagues at the University of Massachusetts Medical Center in Worcester, Massachusetts. The medical literature now contains many reports of individuals, including those with cancer, fibromyalgia, panic attacks, and mild or moderate depression, who reported benefits from learning to practice mindfulness meditation in the interest of health and stress reduction.

In one intriguing study published in 2003 in the medical

journal *Psychosomatic Medicine*, Richard Davidson, Jon Kabat-Zinn, and their colleagues taught a group of small-business employees the skills of mindfulness-based stress reduction in a class over a period of several weeks. They compared the group who meditated with a control group that did not learn or practice mindfulness skills.

The investigators found that there were significant increases in activity in the left frontal region of the brain in the group that meditated compared to the group of non-meditators. Previous studies have shown that such increases in left-sided frontal brain activation correlate with self-reports of increased positive feelings and reduced anxiety.

In addition, the group that meditated demonstrated a stronger immune response to flu vaccine compared to the nonmeditators.

It appears, in this group at least, that the activity of meditation actually promoted significant and measurable physiological changes in brain and body, changes associated with positive feelings and a healthier immune system.

You will find practices in this book to instruct you in strengthening your innate capacity to be mindful. You may even develop a personal meditation practice with the support of some of the practices. As you learn to "breathe mindfully for about a minute" (or for as long as you like!), you give yourself a chance to gain the health benefits now being reported in medical literature for those who practice meditation.

YOUR KEYS TO FIVE GOOD MINUTES
Presence, Intention, and Wholeheartedness

Five good minutes means inhabiting the present moment with awareness, setting clear intentions, and acting whole-heartedly.

Mindfulness: Your Doorway to the Present Moment

"Breathe mindfully for about a minute." "Listen mindfully for about a minute." "Tune in mindfully to your body sensations for about a minute."

You will see these suggestions and others related to mindfulness as you work with the practices in this book. What does it mean to be "mindful"?

Mindfulness is a word for an awareness that all human beings are capable of. This awareness is often likened to a mirror: it reflects whatever comes before it accurately and completely. In other words, you and all other human beings have the capacity for accurate reflection of any experience, including your own inner life of thoughts, feelings, and sensations. Mindfulness is *not* about having more thoughts, but instead is an ability to know when thoughts are happening. It is not thinking at all, but is a simple awareness that recognizes and contains thinking.

Attention is key to being mindful. When you are asked to breathe mindfully for about a minute or to listen mindfully, what you do is pay attention on purpose to the breath sensations or to the sounds in and around you. In fact, being mindful is really about paying attention in a particular way to things you may never have paid attention to before (and to things you have, only in a different way).

The *way* you pay attention is very important.

Being mindful means paying attention without judging or seeking to change anything about what is happening. *Just paying attention*. No agenda, no prejudice.

And embedded in this way of attending are the energies of kindness and compassion. This means that as you practice being mindful, you allow a feeling of friendliness and welcome to support your attention. You practice meeting any experience in a warm and friendly way.

If all of this talk about attention and mindfulness sounds curious, abstract, or difficult, don't worry. It's easier than you might think.

How Being Mindful Might Help You Be Present

You may ask, why would paying attention mindfully be a key to being more present in the moment? Recall for a moment a time when you were not present. Some call it "going on automatic pilot." You realize at some later time that you have actually missed some important event or experience because your attention—your "mind"—was elsewhere.

Another common situation is that people become stuck in a busy mind. They want to relax, but their mind keeps spinning thoughts and stories in an obsessive, out-of-control way.

Well, what happens when you go on automatic pilot or become hijacked by a racing mind is that you have probably become absorbed in your thoughts, feelings, and reactions to what is happening. You may have even developed an identity based on the thoughts and stories you tell yourself, something like, "I am such an anxious person." Or, "I am a person who gets bored easily." "I am (this)…" "I am (that)…" "I am (whatever)…"

As this absorption and identification strengthens, ghosts from the past and worries about the future populate and impact the present moment. You can become confused, lost, even at war, right here in the present moment. Very distracted. Probably unhappy.

By learning to establish mindfulness, you give yourself an escape hatch from the habitual energies of identification and the struggle with whatever is upsetting you at the present moment. You give yourself a more spacious and open place from which to relate to any experience, here, in this moment.

The present moment is where we live and where our lives happen. It is the only place change and transformation can happen. When you are on automatic pilot or hijacked or distracted by upset or worry, your effectiveness and availability for living are diminished.

So, by learning how to bring sensitive attention, receptive awareness, and a kind and open heart here to the present moment, you can actually break the habitual energy of identifying with past and future and change your relationship to what is happening inside and outside your skin.

This is why the *first* minute of your five good minutes is to establish mindfulness.

While you can pay attention and become mindful of literally anything, it is very useful to have a method or practice of mindfulness that you can call on whenever you need it. In this book, we offer mindfulness of breathing and mindful listening as two such anchors for your mindfulness practice. Brief, easy-to-follow instructions for each of these practices follow. Feel free to refer back to these instructions whenever you wish.

Instructions for Mindful Breathing

Whenever you wish to practice mindful breathing, acknowledge to yourself that that is what you are about to do. Say something to yourself like, "Now I am practicing mindful breathing." Remember, you can practice in any posture: sitting, walking, lying down, or standing.

As you begin, recall that being mindful means opening and receiving experience and not trying to change it.

Mindfulness means holding the attitude of kindness and not practicing ill will toward anything arising in your awareness. Without judging it or trying to change anything about it, just let the experience you focus upon (in this case the breath sensations) come to you and stay as long as it wants.

When there is pain or frustration, doubt or worry, meet it with compassion, softness, and kindness instead of rejecting or judging it or yourself in any way.

1. If it helps, softly close your eyes as you begin your meditation.

2. Now, gently bring your attention to the sensations of the breath, the in-breath and the out-breath, as they arise, change, and fade in your body. Let your attention be soft yet focused at the place in your body where it is easiest for you to feel the direct sensation of the breath as it moves. This could be the tip of your nose, your mouth, your chest, your abdomen, or a combination of these. It can be helpful to narrow your focus to a small point once you've found the general location for feeling your breath.

3. As best you can, just relax and sharpen your atten-

tion on the point where you feel the breath. Begin to notice the details and nuances of each in-breath, each out-breath, and the space between breaths. Just relax and let the sensations come to you. Let each sensation stay as long as it needs to. Kindly welcome and allow it to just be. No need to control or change it in any way.

4. It may help to remember that your body knows how to breathe. Let it do what it knows while you pay attention and relax into the constant flow of changing breath sensations.

5. When your attention moves or your mind wanders, try to remember that you haven't done anything wrong. You have not made a mistake. This is just the movement of the untrained mind. Notice where your attention has gone, and gently bring it back to the sensations of this breath. You will probably have to bring your attention back from somewhere else many, many times. That's okay. You are training your attention to stay longer in one place each time you bring it back.

6. Instead of becoming caught up in a sense of struggle over attention moving back and forth from

breath sensations to other experiences, it can be helpful to simply "let the breath back in" when you realize your attention is not on the breath. There really isn't much you have to do to redirect attention—just relax and open to the sensations of the breath, letting them come back "in" and back to you.

7. When thoughts, sounds, or other sensations happen, you don't have to fight them. You don't have to follow them, either. Just let them be. Let them go.

8. Continue practicing with gentle and steady attention focused on the direct sensations of your breath. Kindly and gently let the breath sensations back in whenever something else draws your attention. As you practice, let go of all other burdens. Set them down for the time of this meditation. Rest in the ease arising as you softly hang your attention on the flow of breath sensations and any other experiences that may float in and out. Rest in any sense of silence or stillness that you feel.

9. Let the meditation support you. There is nowhere else to be, nothing else to do, no one to become for the time of this meditation.

10. When you are ready to end your meditation period, shift your focus from the breath sensations, open your eyes, and move gently.

Instructions for Mindful Listening

1. For listening mindfully, follow the same instructions as for mindful breathing, only let the sounds in and around you be the focus of your attention instead of the breath sensations.

2. No need to control the sounds, no need to choose one over another. Just let all the sounds come to you and wash over and through you like waves.

3. Bring an ever more sensitive, accepting, and kind attention to the sounds and to the spaces between the sounds. Notice the soft sounds and the loud ones, the pleasant ones and the unpleasant ones. Let them all be just as they are. Try to welcome each one. Coming to you in its own way and at its own speed. Leaving in its own time.

4. When your attention moves to something else besides sounds, remember that you have not done anything wrong. You haven't made any mistake.

Just as you did with mindful breathing, just relax and let the sounds back in. Let them back in as many times as you need to, always with kindness and patience for them and for yourself.

5. As you practice, you may begin to notice a sense of inner stillness and silence that contains and surrounds all the sounds. If this happens, let yourself abide and rest there more and more. Let the sounds and all experience flow through that stillness and silence.

6. As you continue to practice and as mindfulness grows sharper, you may begin to notice the very beginning of some sounds, how they change, and the precise moment of the ending of the sound. You may begin to notice how there is space before and after the sound. Play with being surprised and even more curious about the interplay of sound and silence as you become more and more mindful.

7. Practice for as long as you like.

8. When you are ready to end your practice, kindly shift your focus from the sounds and the silence, and move gently.

Setting Intention: Making Sure You Are Going in the Right Direction

Your second "good minute" of the five good minutes invites you to set a clear intention.

For example, "May this practice help me feel more relaxed and less stressed."

By making a simple statement like this to yourself at the beginning of an activity, you help to focus your energy and engage more fully in what you're doing.

Setting an intention is a way of pointing yourself in a direction. It is a way of targeting an important value, quality, or goal.

Setting intention can be done skillfully or unskillfully. For instance, it is probably not so skillful or effective to be rigid or greedily attached to an outcome when you set your intention. It's more important to be realistic and kind with yourself and with life as you follow in the direction your intention is pointing at.

For example, if your intention is to feel more relaxed and less stressed, don't get caught up in demanding 100 percent relaxation in just five minutes. Don't fall into judging and doubting, which can make you feel more stressed!

And it's probably not skillful to make your intention, no matter how uplifting, something else on your "to do" list—something else you must achieve at all costs!

An intention is more like a friendly guide. Used skillfully, it can show you a new landscape and lead to new discoveries.

It helps if you acknowledge from the beginning that important changes take time. Now your intention (to be more relaxed, for example) can be thought of as a direction you are choosing to move in. Whatever practice you're using to become more relaxed is a way you have for stepping onto the path and moving in the direction you have chosen.

Your intention is a clear and explicit statement of a value, quality, or goal that is important to you in your life. By stating your intention, you have opened the door for a profound shift in the direction of your goal.

Acting Wholeheartedly: The Key to Getting the Most from Any Practice

To act wholeheartedly means to do something with all of

your attention and energy. Total commitment. No doubts. No holding back.

The last piece of your five good minutes is to do your practice wholeheartedly. Specifically, this means doing whatever your practice directs completely. Whether the instructions call for laughing out loud or shaking your body or paying attention to your inner life or the words of another, do it with as much commitment as you possibly can!

You may find that you have to practice and experiment with being wholehearted. For a variety of reasons much of our activity in life is not done with complete attention or real commitment. So, as you begin to work with the practices in this book, give yourself some room to grow and to explore the landscape of each practice. And, to support being wholehearted, please remember the following:

You don't have to do all the practices.

You don't have to like all the practices.

You don't have to do them in any specific order.

Relax and enjoy them! The practices are on *your* side. They are *here for you*!

To get the most out of your five good minutes, it's probably best for you to browse through the different practices and begin with the ones that resonate with you, the ones that seem especially appealing or are just right for a specific situation happening right now in your life.

As you become more comfortable with particular practices and the principles of five good minutes, you will see how different ones fit into the diverse corners and changing situations of your life.

As you do your practices, you will probably notice that it is easier to be wholehearted if you let go of any attachment to outcome. In fact, the more you let go of trying to change, the more you maximize your chances for change and growth! This paradox is true of most (if not all) of the practices in this book. In the realm of change, growth, and transformation, the more you reach for something, the farther away it gets. The more you relax and open, the more possibilities can emerge. So let go of trying to change anything or to make anything special happen. Just dive in and enjoy what happens as you actually experience your practice.

IN CONCLUSION

Whatever you call your work, you would probably agree that when it goes well, it's a joy. When work isn't going well, it is many things, but not joyful!

What if the joy could be greater?

What if the difficult times could be met differently?

What if you could discover a fresh and richer sense of connection and affection for living as your life's journey proceeds through your workplace?

The intention of this book is to offer every working person friendly new options, new choices, and new possibilities in their work that may, in turn, inform and enrich their own unique and precious journey through life.

It is our deepest hope that you will find more joy, greater ease, improved health and safety, and richer rewards as you explore *Five Good Minutes at Work*.

PART TWO

THE
PRACTICES

Doing Your Work
More Effectively

THE SAME RIVER TWICE?

EACH MOMENT has its own wisdom waiting to be discovered.

We live only in the present moment. Everything happens now, here.

When you find yourself complaining about "the same old routine" or you're feeling bored or stuck, resentful or mistreated, stop and try a different approach.

1. Breathe, listen, or move mindfully for about a minute.

2. Set your intention. For example, "May this practice bring me ease and help me feel more alive."

3. Bring attention to the details of what you are doing. Notice sensations, sounds, and scents as they occur.

4. Acknowledge your thoughts and feelings, no matter how mean or harsh. If you're feeling any upset

or distress, practice kindness and patience with those feelings and yourself.

5. Reconnect with the "routine" activity. Consider how things have changed from the last time you did it. Note that you can never do it again exactly this way. "You cannot step in the same river twice," as the saying goes.

6. How does your life flow through this place, this work, on this day? Does acknowledging changing conditions help you cherish the life appearing here and now?

SHAKE OFF MORNING GROGGINESS

IF YOU didn't get a good night's sleep or spent most of the night trying to find a comfortable sleeping position, then morning grogginess can leave you feeling depleted and unfocused. Since you probably can't take a day off to catch up on that much-needed rest, the following exercise will help restore your energy.

1. Use this moment first to ground yourself by taking three deep breaths, bringing in and then releasing the air slowly and methodically.

2. Be seated and close your eyes, if possible, and imagine you're taking a restorative power nap. Let your mind relax and your body go limp.

3. During your "nap," recall the best night's sleep that you can remember. All is at ease. The house is quiet. The kids are dreaming. Your partner isn't snoring. Not a sound can be heard for miles around you. Upon awakening, you feel ready to take on your day.

4. Say aloud or to yourself, "When I open my eyes, I will feel refreshed and invigorated. I will feel focused and alert. I will be ready to take on this workday with new vigor."

Recharge yourself with a few five-minute power naps when you feel sleepy during your workday.

3

RING THE SAFETY BELL

APPROACHING A risky situation or task as you work requires care and attention. Whether the risk is physical, emotional, or psychological, you can learn to ring your "safety bell" and let mindfulness support and protect you.

1. Gently begin to notice when you feel increased vigilance or apprehension for an approaching task or situation.

2. Imagine an inner safety bell going off to mark the situation. Let the bell's sound be beautiful, clear, and unmistakable.

3. Begin focusing careful attention on what is happening within you and in the outer world. Take some mindful breaths to anchor your attention and to support some ease.

4. Affirm yourself. For example, "Paying more relaxed attention protects and supports me."

5. Look closer, start the work, and let yourself feel what is happening. As you proceed, notice all accompanying sensations and feelings, inside and out. Let mindful breathing support you, holding you and the work with a sense of ease and spaciousness.

6. When the job is done, let the "all clear" bell sound.

4

TOO MUCH WORK, TOO LITTLE TIME

FOR MANY of us, there simply isn't enough time in the day to get all our work done. Despite your extraordinary efforts to multitask, the in-box fills up, the voice messages multiply, and additional unforeseen tasks get added to your pile. You may feel overwhelmed, fatigued, and anxious about the impossibility of meeting these pressing demands. The next few minutes are dedicated to returning your consciousness to the present moment, which starts with exactly where you are. This mindful meditation will help keep you on track.

1. Begin by centering yourself in the here and now. You may want to take a few breaths or roll your shoulders to loosen up any nagging tension.

2. Remind yourself that today is only one day. You are only one person. You have only so much time to get so much done. You may not catch up or complete everything in one day—and that's okay.

3. Take one last deep breath, and on the slow exhale say aloud, "I will accomplish a great deal today, and tomorrow is a new day."

CENTER OF ATTENTION

Do you ever feel scattered or "not all there" at work? Do you find yourself making errors, dropping things, feeling dull or irritable and unfocused?

Whenever you notice such feelings of distraction and inattention, try the following practice to center your attention and recover a sense of connection with the present moment.

1. Begin moving in any way, and bring mindful attention to your body.

2. Move gently and slowly for at least a minute and focus your attention mindfully on the variety and changing quality of sensations in your body.

3. Expand the focus to include your breath sensations, and breathe mindfully for a few breaths.

4. Now include any thoughts, noticing their tone of voice. You don't have to follow the thoughts or add to them, and you don't have to fight them either. Just let them be.

5. Finally, open to everything else that is happening—sounds, scents, tastes—letting them come in as you make room for each one, softly and kindly.

6. When you wish, bring your focus back to your work. How do you feel?

THE BIGGER PICTURE

WHETHER YOU work behind a desk or service counter, outside, or bedside, you may get burdened by incessant interruptions that derail your attempts to stay focused on the job at hand. The phone rings, a customer complains, or you misplace something, all of which decrease your productivity and can lead to stress. The following practice will help you quiet the impact of these stressful disruptions.

1. Acknowledge, first, what is causing the stress—a deadline, muscle tension, annoyance, or fear of failure.

2. Tell yourself, "This is not life-threatening. I will survive, and this moment will pass."

3. Inhale a slow, deep breath, letting your belly expand as you inhale. On the exhale, let your eyes leisurely wander around the entire circumference of your present environment. Allow your vision to

take in all that's around you—the table, architecture, art, or sky.

4. In this moment, become aware that there is more than one way to see any situation, no matter how awful it might seem right now.

MIND YOUR POSITION

INJURIES, EITHER from sudden or repetitive motions, can result if you aren't paying attention closely or often enough to your body's position or condition.

This practice can help you develop more body awareness, helping you work more safely and toward better health.

1. Breathe or listen mindfully for about a minute.

2. Set your intention. For example: "May I protect and help my body by paying closer attention to it."

3. Gently bring mindful attention to the direct sen-

sations flowing through your body. Let them be. Allow each to come into awareness at its own pace. Now relax, soften, and let each one in.

4. Notice the quality of each sensation—vibration, heat, contraction, pulsing, and so on.

5. Allow your body to move or adjust as it wishes while you kindly observe and receive the sensations.

6. Honor any stretching or other movement your body needs.

PERSONAL BALANCING ACT

NO MATTER what your profession, your personal life can sometimes distract you from the work at hand. Perhaps you're worried about your child or an ill family member or a recent divorce. No one is immune to these concerns, and yet in the fast-paced business world, few of us can afford to drop our jobs and adequately tend to our daily personal worries. But there's no reason why we can't both acknowledge our personal life and be present for our work duties. Try this private ritual for maintaining a healthy balance between both your worlds.

1. First, acknowledge what's going in your life outside of work.

2. Take this moment to give yourself the comfort and tenderness that you need. Say aloud, "I am worried about _____. In this moment, I feel _____. There will be time eventually to get through this."

3. Take an easy breath. Remind yourself throughout your workday to move gently, to not push yourself too hard, and that there will be time to attend to your personal concerns.

9

COURAGE

TOO OFTEN a difficult or challenging work situation evokes feelings of fear or self-doubt. Such feelings can derail or impair your ability to work effectively.

Real courage acknowledges fear, includes it, and acts effectively anyway.

When you feel yourself becoming derailed by fear or doubt, try the following practice.

1. Breathe or listen mindfully for about a minute.

2. Set your intention. For example, "May this practice give me strength and courage."

3. Make room for any upset you feel. Name it. Allow it. Breathe mindfully with it.

4. Imagine that your body—outer and inner—is vast and steady, like a mountain.

5. The mountain withstands storms, fires, everything. Your upset is only a passing storm to the mountain.

6. If you like, repeat a word like "courage" or "steady" or "unshakable" quietly to yourself.

7. Feel the solid earth beneath you and the strong mountain within you.

IO

LET IT ALL GO

WHEN YOU'RE angry or frustrated, your thoughts can run amok. One negative thought leads to another and then another, threatening to spiral out of control into the darkest regions of hopelessness. These depressing worries are very difficult to unwind from and can disturb your concentration at work. A mindfulness meditation will help you reconnect to what's most important to you and refocus on the task at hand.

1. When you find yourself in a negative mental-feedback loop, ask yourself, "Are these endless thoughts improving my situation or helping me in any way? Is it possible that there may be other ways to think about my circumstance?"

2. Take a brief moment to ground yourself by looking at an object in your environment that makes you feel calm, such as a plant or a personal photo. Now focus your attention on your breath. Gently observe your inhalation and exhalation.

3. When your attention wanders again toward unhealthy negative patterns throughout the day, just shift and refocus your attention back to your breath and the calming object.

II

DON'T LIKE WHAT YOU'RE DOING?

AN OLD saying goes, "If you can't get out of it, get behind it!"

How much is lost when you are fighting within yourself against the very activity you're trying to accomplish?

Next time you find yourself fighting, try the following practice.

1. Breathe or listen mindfully for about a minute.

2. Set your intention. For example, "May this practice bring me more peace and joy."

3. Listen mindfully to your inner voices. Are they loud, angry, afraid—what? Remember that you don't have to fight them, and you don't have to follow them.

4. When you notice feelings of aversion or ill will toward anything, gently name them.

5. Breathe mindfully for a few more breaths. Imagine that the ill will leaves you on each breath out.

6. Refocus on your work. Can you see something valuable there? Can you meet it with interest?

12

FIVE-STAR VALUE

MOST OF us need to receive some amount of appreciation for the work that we do. The best form may come in a pay raise, a letter of appreciation, or a compliment from your supervisor. But what if you feel that others don't value your work? Over time, this perception can be very discouraging, and it can damage your self-esteem. This exercise will boost your sense of self-worth—because when you feel good about yourself, your work tends to improve.

- *Take this moment to first acknowledge all the things you do at work that keep everything flowing smoothly. In fact, without you, there might be total chaos—phones ringing off the hook, jammed fax machines, lost files, ignored customers, and so on.*

- *Close your eyes and remember that appreciation starts from within. Be mindful of giving yourself daily praise: You work hard and have many talents. You are more than the value of your paycheck. You make an important contribution.*

13

FRESH EYES

IT'S EASY to become unconscious of and disconnected from the people and things that surround you in everyday working (and home) life.

There is a cost for this inattention and disconnection. It includes loss of motivation, feelings of boredom, even neglect of responsibilities.

Try motivating yourself by seeing something *new* in everyday situations.

1. Pick any situation or task that comes up repeatedly. The next time you encounter it, just before engaging, close your eyes and breathe or listen mindfully for about a minute.

2. Set your intention. For example, "May this practice help me see with fresh eyes."

3. Breathe or listen mindfully a bit longer.

4. Open your eyes to the situation. Look with interest and curiosity, as if seeing it for the first time.

5. Now look even more closely. Note objects, people, space, activity.

6. Let friendliness and curiosity support you. What do you see now?

14

DRAIN THE STRAIN

FEW OF us think of our work space as a refuge for meditation. But even in the sometimes hectic realm of work, you can find inner and outer space for peace. The next exercise can be done at your desk, the office hallway, or even outside.

1. In a standing position, inhale slowly and deeply from the diaphragm. Exhale, and let your jaw, tongue, arms, and shoulders go completely loose. Feel the heaviness throughout your entire body, pulsating down your arms and legs as though they were hollow drainpipes.

2. With each inhale, imagine gusts of refreshing air flushing the tension through these pipes and pushing it out at your fingertips and toes with each exhale.

3. Shake out your body thoroughly by jiggling your shoulders to each side and swinging your arms to and fro. You can also jiggle each leg, one at a time.

When you recognize your stress levels maxing out, take five minutes to decompress, unwind, and shake out your mounting tension.

15

FEELING RUSHED?

A WISE person once said, "Be quick but don't hurry."

Feeling rushed drives one to hurry. Constant hurrying can lead to mistakes, accidents, and even burnout.

Try the following practice when you find yourself hurrying. It can help you become more relaxed—and quicker!

1. Whenever you feel rushed, stop and breathe, listen, or move mindfully.

2. Affirm yourself. For example, "I remember that I have all the support I need."

3. Center mindful attention on your breath and body sensations for a few breaths. Reconnect with your body, and allow the flow of all sensations.

4. Notice any thoughts or chatter in your mind. Acknowledge the mental story without fighting or following it.

5. Attend mindfully to breath or body sensations for a few more breaths.

6. Recall a specific source of personal strength or support, and repeat your affirmation.

7. Return to work with a lighter step and a refreshed spirit.

16

TAKE A HIKE

IN TODAY'S sedentary lifestyle, we often don't get enough exercise. But even a short, gentle stroll can alleviate pent-up stress and remind you of the healing force of moving your body. Just before lunch, give yourself permission to get outside and go for a walk, take a hike, or jog around the vicinity. The fresh air alone will do you some good.

- *On your walk, take five minutes to be mindful of your natural surroundings—the birds, plants, insects, wind, and clouds. Even if you work in the middle of a city, the natural world is all around you.*

- *With each step, you are distancing yourself from all your work obligations and stress. You are leaving behind your extra burden.*

- *With each breath, notice the world around you—people, places, sculptures, and parks.*

- *When it comes time to return, with every step you take toward your job site, become increasingly aware of the calming power of being outside.*

17

YOUR REAL IMPACT

Do you ever wonder if your job is really important? Do you think that it's not connected with the rest of your life?

Well, what you see is what you get!

Try seeing *more* with the following practice.

1. Breathe, listen, or move mindfully for about a minute.

2. Set your intention. For example, "May this practice awaken joy in me."

3. Sit and breathe or listen mindfully for a bit longer.

4. Reflect on your work. What do you do, exactly? Who benefits? Who depends on you? Look deeply at these questions.

5. Breathe or listen mindfully for a few breaths more.

6. Ask yourself, "What matters most dearly to me? How does benefiting others reflect my own core values? Where are these things in my work?"

7. Listen for all the responses. Let yourself be surprised!

18

JUNK BREAK

EXCESSIVE STRESS can lead us to make immediately gratifying but unhealthy food choices, resulting in heartburn, indigestion, and exhaustion. The next time you become aware of your desire to wolf down a candy bar or bag of chips when your stress level rises, try this exercise to help you make healthy food choices.

1. Take a moment to acknowledge your hunger or your sweet tooth. Feel how it is trying to convince you that an unhealthy snack will make you feel better.

2. Stress can adversely affect your decision-making power. Tell yourself, "Nutritious food choices will reduce my stress load and improve my ability to think clearly."

3. Visualize eating a healthy snack, such as apples and walnuts, yogurt and blueberries, carrots and hummus, or celery and peanut butter. Imagine how good your body will feel from eating something nourishing and wholesome.

Make the effort to select good snacks or pick up healthy snacks after work so you always have something delicious and nutritious on hand.

19

YOU DO GOOD WORK!

FOR MANY reasons, people seem programmed to notice only what goes wrong, what was missed, or how they failed.

Knowing and enjoying what you did well is also important.

Try the following to appreciate your *good* work.

1. Pick a time and place when you will not be disturbed.

2. Breathe or listen mindfully for about a minute.

3. Set your intention. For example, "May this practice show me the good I do."

4. Breathe or listen mindfully for a few more breaths.

5. Recall a job, task, or situation when you succeeded or did well. Notice your contributions. See how others benefited from your kindness, intelligence, and special skills.

6. Open and allow yourself to enjoy any feelings of satisfaction and confidence you notice.

7. Let the good feelings fill and support you.

A MATTER OF HEART

THERE'S NOTHING more uncomfortable than starting your work morning with a personal-life stressor clawing at your mind. The following practice will restore inner balance and calm, which will initiate the process of healing what ails the heart.

1. Begin by placing your hand over your heart with the purpose of locating your heartbeat.

2. Once you've found your rhythm, breathe slowly and mindfully into your abdomen. Notice how your breathing can affect your heart rate. Under stress, we tend to take shallow breaths, inadequately filling our lungs and body with oxygen.

3. Now breathe more deeply and abundantly, filling your chest cavity with air. How has your rhythm changed or relaxed?

During times of immediate personal-life strain, you may build up physical and emotional tension in your heart. By reconnecting with your heartbeat, you can release excess tension and restore a feeling of centeredness.

21

KEYS TO EFFECTIVE ACTION

A SUCCESSFUL person knows that effective action is built on three key elements: clarity, simplicity, and focus.

Try the following practice to support your success!

1. Breathe or listen mindfully for about a minute.

2. Set your intention. For example, "May this practice strengthen my effectiveness."

3. Breathe or listen mindfully for a few more breaths.

4. Focus on a task or project.

5. First ask, "What is the main thing being asked of me here?" Listen with curiosity for any response. The answer may be very obvious.

6. Next ask, "What is the simplest way to do what is asked?" Listen deeply, trusting your inner guidance and wisdom.

7. Now ask, "Where do I begin to be successful?" Be patient. Let the answer come to you without over-analyzing it, and get started.

8. Clarity, simplicity, and focus. Keep your keys to success handy!

22

MENTAL VACATION

When was the last time you let your mind drift out to the unknown? The last time you let yourself stare off into outer space? At work, we rarely give ourselves permission to take mental-health holidays. Let's do it right now.

- *Get in a comfortable position and close your eyes, if*

possible. This is your opportunity to slow down, quiet your mind, and let go of all those urgent, pressing work matters.

- Consciously steer your mind away from your job or obligations and toward a personal oasis or paradise spot. You are free to empty your mind of all thoughts and feelings and just let yourself be. For the next few minutes, just drift in your imagined oasis.

- As you drift mentally farther out to this quiet space, imagine returning to your work with the feeling of serenity, like tiny beads of water still clinging to your skin.

23

SERENITY

Do you ever wish that you could meet work demands with more serenity—even for a little while? Would things go better if you could?

Serenity is associated with feelings of calm, peace, ease, and steadiness.

Such feelings may be no farther away than taking the time to apply your imagination and wholehearted attention.

1. Pick a place that offers some privacy.

2. Breathe or listen mindfully for about a minute.

3. Set your intention. For example, "May this practice bring me calm and steadiness."

4. Imagine yourself in a beautiful and serene spot in nature—a quiet forest, a high mountain meadow, beside a gently flowing stream, or anyplace you like.

5. Let this serene place begin to fill all your senses. What do you feel? Hear? See? Smell? Taste? Allow yourself to drink it all in. Let serenity fill and surround you.

6. Stay as long as you like. Return whenever you wish. Bring serenity back to work.

24

EMPTY YOUR POCKETS OF TENSION

WHETHER YOU suffer from the occasional headache, knee pain, cramps, or backache, physical pain anywhere in the body can put you in a bad mood and hinder your productivity level at work. You may feel frustrated and limited by the simplest task, or you may find working with others nearly impossible. Chronic pain exacerbates the problem, and you may experience your pain like a ball and chain. Try this upper-body stretch for maintaining flexibility and giving your body a chance to release those pockets of stored tension.

1. From a standing position with your feet shoulder-width apart, breathe deeply into your belly for several breaths, allowing relaxation to flow through your body with each exhalation.

2. Begin now by reaching toward the ceiling with your right arm, keeping your left side completely relaxed, and gently bend to your left while main-

taining a straight arm. Hold the stretch for thirty seconds, and remember to breathe.

3. Relax and then switch sides, reaching with your left arm and bending to your right. Repeat three to five times on each side and frequently throughout the day whenever you feel soreness or fatigue.

A SEAT FOR YOUR SORROWS

SOME DAYS, no matter how hard you try to keep it all together on the outside, you may feel like you're crumbling on the inside. You become a leaky faucet of emotions. Everything triggers your sore spot, and you're on the verge of tears at the drop of a pen. The more you force the feelings downward, the more easily they slice through to the surface. Instead of fighting it, take some time to sit with the discomfort.

- *Start by admitting your internal feelings of distress. You may be struggling with personal issues or an employment-*

related dilemma or sadness over the state of affairs of our world.

- Imagine pulling up another chair for your extra burden of sadness. Offer your emotions a seat, then prop them up with extra fluffy pillows and a warm afghan. You may not be able to shed all the troublesome feelings, but you can create a comfortable and safe space for your feelings to reside.

The more tender and accommodating you can be with your emotions, the more easily they will heal and the more validated you will come to feel.

Reducing Stress
At Work

26

CALL FOR SUPPORT

STRESS CAN easily lead to disturbing feelings and thoughts on the job.

Learn to meet any disturbing or painful feelings and thoughts by cheering your mind and opening your heart, using the energies of gratitude and appreciation.

1. When you are feeling any kind of inner upset or distress, turn compassionate and mindful attention to it and yourself.

2. Breathe mindfully for about a minute.

3. Shift your attention and begin to name things or people or conditions that support and help you.

4. Let your focus expand as you become more and more specific. For example, "I have good colleagues." Or, "I can get the information I need." Or, "I have a family who loves me."

5. Notice how gratitude and appreciation can grow

within you. Remember the supports you do have. Let the naming of your benefactors and strengths awaken feelings of confidence and ease. Receive and rest in the energy of gratitude and the recognition of your supports.

6. When you're ready, revisit the situation that caused the upset. Open to any new insights or understandings that may come.

ONLY CHANGE IS CERTAIN

JOB INSTABILITY affects everyone at some point in his or her life. You may lie awake at night worrying about being laid off too, and agonizing over how you'll find another job. With the added stress of a mortgage, car payments, a kid in college, and endless bills, you've got more than your share of burden to bear. The following visualization is a guide for reminding you that despite these stressors, optimism can be a powerful tool during times of uncertainty.

- Take a brief moment to recognize that you are exactly where you need to be and doing just what you're supposed be doing.

- Tell yourself, "Today I have a job and an income. I will do the best I can today but I cannot control tomorrow." There are few things in our lives that promise absolute certainty and permanence.

- After several deep breaths, visualize yourself at ease with any job, whether it's the one you have now, a reconfigured one, or even an entirely new one. Imagine you are meeting new people, feeling challenged by new tasks, and open to new opportunities. Carry this picture in your mind throughout your workday, easing uncomfortable feelings of instability.

28

ILLNESS PATROL

WE'VE ALL done it. Dragged ourselves to work even though we're experiencing flu-like symptoms, or perhaps the worst case of allergies has just kicked in. You're congested, achy, and sniffly, but you show up to work anyway. You just can't bear the thought of getting more behind, and they need you, you insist. If you're lucky, you'll be able to quit in the middle of the shift and head straight for bed. But what if you can't? What if you can't afford to miss even one day's work? Take five minutes to be mindful of every course of action that you can take to heal your illness. Below are reminders to be gentle with yourself and to move slowly and cautiously when you're sick.

- *Keep a cup of calming herbal tea beside you all day.*

- *Get some fresh air and feel the sun on your face.*

- *Give yourself permission to sit down, get comfortable, close your eyes, and remember that even a few minutes of rest will conserve energy.*

- *Replenish your body with fluids, and flush out that bug with at least eight to ten glasses of water per day.*

- *If you have vitamin C or a multivitamin on hand, take it.*

Slow down your usual pace when you're sick. Be conscious when your pace feels frenzied, and remind yourself frequently that you can ask for help if you need it.

29

SHAKE IT OFF

YOUR MIND and body are deeply connected. Your body accumulates and carries stress and tensions. And your body will let you know it!

Try the following for fun and for stress reduction.

1. When you feel stressed, take a moment to kindly acknowledge the feelings of stress.

2. Now, take a few mindful breaths.

3. Shift your attention to your body. Tune in to the sensations flowing through you. Notice especially where the sensations seem the strongest or most uncomfortable.

4. Whether standing, sitting, or lying down, be sure you are balanced and well supported. Then let your body start to move and gently shake wherever the stress feels the heaviest.

5. Stretch, move, and shake it off!

6. As you shake, you may want to add some fun and surprising sounds to the movement. Just remember not to frighten or upset others within earshot.

7. Enjoy!

30

FREEDOM FROM THE VALLEY
OF "WHAT IF"

ARE YOU someone who lives in the land of "what if"? What if that job doesn't come through? What if I don't make my sales quota this month? What if my order comes late? The more you try to analyze every possible variable, the more disastrous the scenarios can become. You may feel terrible anxiety, fretting over every conceivable negative outcome. The next time you notice yourself cascading down the white waters of "what if," try this guided visualization.

- *Close your eyes and reconnect with the rhythm of your breathing. Take a few deep breaths, slackening your body with each exhale.*

- *You've been here before, you think, buried beneath every what-if-this, what-if-that thought, and there are very few things you can ultimately do to change the result. Repeat to yourself, "I may not be able to control the outcome, but I can work with what is happening at this exact moment."*

- *Visualize aligning yourself with the best possible circumstances. Make a mental list of one to three optimal outcomes, such as, "Everything will be okay" or "This is the best I can do, and it will have to do." Life does occasionally surprise you, and you are welcoming a positive situation in the end.*

Letting go of the outcome is a practice that takes time and patience but can free your mind for a better connection to the present, working with what's right in front of you now.

3I

THE HABIT BREAK

YOUR WORK break can be a time for many things. Whatever you do, it's important that you are there wholeheartedly and enjoy it as much as possible!

This practice invites you to step back from the momentum of and unconscious reactions to work demands and to recover your connection with what is happening in the present moment. Being more present can help you truly enjoy your break activity.

Apply these skills of connecting, free of habit energy, any time you wish!

1. As you begin your break, breathe or move mindfully for about a minute.

2. Set your intention. For example, "May I be totally present and at ease during this time."

3. Whatever you do next, focus mindfully on one clear detail: the warmth of coffee, the sounds around you, or a beautiful scene, for example.

4. When an insistent thought or memory intrudes, speak kindly to it. Assure it that you will return later and take good care of it.

5. When it is time, bring the same clear focus and kind regard back into work activity.

32

WHOOPS!

UNDER EXTREME stress, even a minor mistake can send you reeling over the edge, grasping for some spare sanity. Some days, you might feel like you're all thumbs, fumbling and dropping items, and wasting precious time while you bumble through your workday. Are you extra hard on yourself when you make a mistake? The next time you berate or punish yourself over your misjudgment, follow this mindful practice for calming your frayed nerves.

- *Ground yourself by relaxing into several slow, rhythmic breaths.*

- *Say aloud or inwardly, "Whoops, I'm human. I'm fallible. I make mistakes just like everyone else. I accept this inevitability."*

- *Consider ways that you can forgive and move on, despite your situation. You may want to forgive yourself in writing, or you may want to seek out reassurance from a coworker or friend. This is your opportunity to relinquish self-blame and punishment and to move more gently and calmly through your workday.*

33

BEAT THE PROCRASTINATOR

PROCRASTINATION plagues us all. For some of us, it comes from a lack of motivation, too much autonomy, or sheer boredom. Still others work better under pressure and put work essentials off to the last minute, which often entails caffeine-fueled cramming at the end. But you don't need to suffer the reckless oversights, frequently overlooked errors, and inexcusable delays of procrastination. Beat the procrastinator with these mindful suggestions.

- *Mark your calendar weeks in advance of crucial deadlines.*

- *Rally other coworkers into preparing their assignments ahead of schedule.*

- *Create a checklist of small tasks that you can begin today that will ensure fewer mistakes and miscalculations toward the end.*

- *Start a new folder for your to-do list. Label it "To do: URGENT" in bold red letters. Keep it on your desk and check it two times a day to remind yourself what's on your plate.*

The efforts you make now, in advance of your deadline, will reduce your stress in the final hours. When procrastination threatens to sabotage the efficacy and accuracy of your work, stay conscious of preparation strategies ahead of time.

FRESH BREATH

"TAKE A deep breath" is always good advice for reducing stress. This practice invites you to combine present-moment awareness with refreshing imagery. It can be very nice to do this practice in an open, natural environment, but it can just as easily be done at the comfort of your desk.

1. Take a comfortable position. Let your belly soften and relax. Gently close your eyes.

2. Breathe mindfully for a few breaths, really opening and letting the sensations come to you.

3. For the rest of this practice, imagine or visualize that each in-breath brings you clean, fresh, and invigorating energy. Picture that life energy filling your entire body.

4. Let each out-breath carry away stress and tension. Let yourself deeply feel the ease and release offered by each out-breath.

5. Ride the waves of in- and out-breaths for as long and as deeply as you like.

6. Finish by opening your eyes and moving gently.

SPEAK UP

DEPENDING ON your personality, temperament, or job status or position, you may encounter the stumbling blocks of needing to speak up for yourself and ask for what you need. Whether you need to request a raise from your boss or ask more from a subordinate, there is nothing simple about giving voice to your needs when you're shy, introverted, or feeling unassertive. Take this moment to enhance your ability to face any situation with self-confidence and assuredness.

1. Start with examining your mental list of exactly what you need and why. For example, "My work duties have increased significantly since I first started this job, and I really need an assistant in order to do my job more effectively."

2. Visualize facing your supervisor and speaking in a clear, calm, and confident tone, describing your current situation and proposed solution. Imagine yourself sounding convincing and competent. See your boss listening intently and openly to your requests.

3. The outcome, you hope, is positive and favorable, but what's even more important is that you practice tapping into your inner powers of persuasion and finally speak up for yourself.

Speaking your truths is a critical part of believing in yourself and establishing confidence.

36

BETTER LATE THAN NEVER

IT'S ONE of those hectic, manic mornings where you've just noticed in your daily planner that an employee meeting started twenty minutes ago. Being late for an important meeting is humiliating and piles on the mental strain. Let's focus on relieving the anxiety and restoring balance and concentration.

1. First, make sure you have what you need to feel prepared for this meeting—notepad, pen, files, paperwork, and so on.

2. Take several very slow, deep breaths. As you inhale through your nose, notice the sensation of cool air through your nostrils. On your exhale, notice the warmth that you release.

3. For the next few moments, take a series of breaths and smile on each exhale. You might say inwardly, "I am right where I need to be now" or "I am present and accounted for."

Though your day may continue at a wild velocity, shift your attention away from how awful you feel about being late toward your ability to be present, to listen, and to be prepared.

37

THE WHOLE TRUTH

It's easy to become lost in the flow of thoughts and "head stuff," forgetting your wholeness and the possibility of wonder and mystery available in each moment.

A quick path to returning to wholeness lies in paying attention mindfully to what is happening in each of your senses.

For fun and discovery, try the following.

1. Breathe or listen mindfully for about a minute.

2. Set your intention. For example, "May this practice help me reconnect with my wholeness."

3. Let your mind and heart soften, and open as much as feels safe to you.

4. Listen mindfully to sounds.

5. Let all sensations in, feeling them with affection.

6. Open your eyes and notice shapes, colors, movement, and the space around you.

7. When thoughts arise, don't fight them, and don't follow them.

8. Relax into any feeling of stillness or spaciousness you notice.

38

YOUR OWN PRIVATE ISLAND

FEW OF us have the luxury of private space at work. Maybe you're in customer-service work, taking calls all day. Or it could be you share an office with paper-thin cubicle walls and no doors. Or maybe you supervise a hundred employees who place countless demands and pressures on you. In your hurried, scattered work shift, you may long for a brief moment of solitude. How can you create this privacy when you rarely get a moment alone?

- *Somewhere between phone calls and delegating orders, slip away for a five-minute break.*

- *Draw an imaginary circle around yourself. This circle marks your own private island of solitude. Within your circle, no one can enter, no one can make demands on you, and no one can disrupt your inner peace and harmony. You may hear outside noises—buses, cars, a lawn mower, cell phones—but they don't have anything to do with you.*

- *Keep this imaginary island with you when you start to feel overwhelmed by the incessant pressures to always be available to others. It's your own private breathing room for safety.*

39

FEELING BORED?

NEED A remedy for the times when you feel bored or impatient?

Try applying *kind attention*.

At work, when boredom visits, experiment with the following.

1. Breathe or listen mindfully for about a minute.

2. Set your intention. For example, "May this practice awaken joy and interest in me."

3. Open to and acknowledge any feeling of impatience or unrest inside. Allow it to come in kindly, not fighting it, and not feeding it.

4. Continue to breathe or listen mindfully.

5. Shift your attention to include everything around you. Look closely, listen carefully, and let even scents and tastes into your awareness.

6. Bring sharper attention especially to the familiar things, to ordinary things, as if you were experiencing them for the first time in your life.

7. What do you notice?

8. How does it feel to connect?

STOP WATCHING THE CLOCK

WHY DO the last couple of hours of your work shift appear to go by excruciatingly slowly, as if time were at a standstill? If you find yourself watching the second hand on the clock or looking for your car keys an hour before you've even finished your tasks, try this exercise for distracting your mind from the endless clock-watching game.

- *Begin by reconnecting with the rhythm of your breathing: inhale and exhale, inhale and exhale. Are you relaxed? Pay attention to your body. Notice the thoughts running through your mind.*

- On your in-breath, say aloud or inwardly, "In this breath, I am drawing myself closer to this moment in time."

- On your out-breath, say aloud or inwardly, "In this breath, I am distancing myself from what the future may or may not bring."

- Prioritize the tasks that are in front of you and visualize the satisfaction of crossing off a few more tasks.

Keeping busy and focused on your immediate assignments will maximize your time and give you a sense of accomplishment at the end of your shift.

41

IT WASN'T ALWAYS THIS WAY

WE'VE ALL been in the position where we feel like our work is killing our spirit, or our job satisfaction is so unbearably low that we're not certain how we can make it through another day. This is called "burnout," and it's the feeling of climbing an enormous mountain of discontent.

The day drags on tediously, and you find little pleasure in any of your usual tasks. You may not be able to change jobs overnight, but you can try a simple, mindful practice that may pick up your mood and engage you more deeply in your routine.

- *Remember when you first started your job? Everything was new and stimulating. You were acquiring unique skills, and the training was challenging. You felt the effects of intellectual and mental growth as you learned to incorporate a new methodology into your repertoire.*

- *Take this time to consider new avenues for asserting yourself. Make a list of possibilities for new skills that you would be interested in obtaining, such as taking a computer programming class, starting a recycling committee, or becoming proficient in a second language.*

With some luck and a good proposal, perhaps your employer will cover the expenses of the new challenge.

42

BEFRIEND YOURSELF

IF ASKED, "Who are your best friends at work?" would you think to include yourself?

There is much to be learned by treating oneself as a good friend.

This practice invites you to explore befriending yourself.

1. Breathe or listen mindfully for about a minute.

2. Set your intention. For example, "May I encourage tolerance and kindness for myself through this practice."

3. Open your attention and welcome any body sensations.

4. Feel the life flowing in your body and imagine speaking to yourself as you would to a good friend—with affection and kindness.

5. Use a word or phrase anyone would appreciate to wish yourself well. For example, "May I be safe... happy...healthy...filled with peace."

6. Put all your heart behind your wish as you speak.

7. Notice and honor whatever you feel.

43

POWER BREAK

MOST OF us are extremely dependent on electronics for the work that we do. You may be required to keep a beeper or cell phone with you at all times, take your laptop when you travel, or monitor an internal company e-mail program all day long. Without these items, your work simply cannot get done. Consider taking five minutes for a silent meditation retreat away from all electronics.

- *Begin by sitting upright, relaxed and alert. Keep your eyes open, with a soft gaze, and place your hands palmside down, gently resting on your thighs. Loosen your facial muscles and jaw, leaving your mouth slightly open. Breathe normally and calmly.*

- *Sitting in silence opens you to a unique experience. Take notice of the simple vibrancy of your immediate sur-*

roundings: *the murmur of distant voices, the hum of passing traffic, the splashes of color around you, the subtle warmth of your hands on your thighs. For a moment, allow your senses to come alive and let your experience in the immediate moment become unfettered and simple.*

44

BREATHE IN STRENGTH AND ENERGY

SOMETIMES you just feel down and low.

If your situation does not allow you to move or take a break to recharge, try the following practice to reenergize!

1. Breathe or listen mindfully for about a minute.

2. Set your intention. For example, "May this practice support and energize me."

3. Breathe mindfully for a few breaths.

4. Imagine each in-breath filling you with light. The light expands into your muscles, your mind, and your heart. With each breath, feel yourself growing warmer and stronger. If you like, repeat the

words "growing stronger" with each in-breath.

5. Continue breathing mindfully.

6. Notice how each out-breath can leave you feeling lighter and more at ease. Try words like: "lighter and brighter, more energy" with each out-breath.

7. Breathe in strength and energy as often as you wish.

RESTORE YOUR NATURAL RHYTHM

UNDER EXTREME stress, there is a tendency to hold your breath. Escalating work demands can cause a shortness of breath. Relentlessly pressing deadlines may push you to the edge of your seat with anxiety, which further obstructs your natural breathing rhythm. The following exercise will assist you in replacing your rocket-fuel stress with peace and serenity.

1. Notice the occasions in your workday when tension rises and when your chest may tighten.

Notice when your breathing becomes irregular or when you're holding your breath.

2. During these times of stress, practice moving more breath into and out of the body, helping your body take in more oxygen. Three long, deep breaths into your belly will work.

3. Let go of the belly breathing and allow your body to breathe naturally and at its own depth and rhythm, until you begin to feel a sense of calm arising.

4. Pay attention to sensations occurring from the body's natural breathing patterns. Are you feeling less anxious? Are you experiencing a loosening and relaxing in your body?

46

DID SOMEONE YELL AT YOU?

If you've been yelled at or belittled on the job, you know that people can be emotionally unintelligent!

Lacking in skills of social and self-awareness and the ability to manage feelings and relationships skillfully, a rude, insensitive person can speak or act in hurtful ways.

When rudeness strikes you, try the following practice.

1. Breathe, listen, or move mindfully for about a minute.

2. Affirm yourself. For example, "That was *not* about me. I know I am okay."

3. Bring compassionate and mindful attention to your inner life. Notice and allow sensations, feelings, and thoughts. Breathe mindfully and let them be, not fighting them and not feeding them.

4. Remember something positive in your life. Affirm that, perhaps saying, "This good thing *is* true."

5. Don't take the experience personally. Remind yourself, "I don't need to carry this further."

6. Breathe or listen mindfully for a few more breaths.

7. When you feel ready, gently offer the rude person forgiveness, and move on.

TENSION TAMER

MANY JOBS require upper-body strength or, at the very least, endurance, whether you work at a computer or in a flower shop or care for the elderly. At first, you may experience mild discomfort in your neck and shoulders, only to be followed by more intensely crippling pain by the end of the day. Reduce your discomfort dramatically by taking frequent, small breaks to practice an exercise to loosen your neck and shoulders.

- *From a standing position or seated at the edge of your chair with your feet shoulder-width apart and leaning your body slightly more forward than your knees, let your arms hang loose at your sides.*

- *Tilting your head back, raise your eyes to the ceiling, slowly looking as far back as you can and mentally marking the spot on the ceiling. Then gradually bring your chin toward your chest. Be gentle with your neck. Return to a relaxed, upright position.*

- *Next, draw both shoulders up toward your earlobes, tightening briefly, and then quickly release and drop your arms loosely at your sides.*

Repeat these exercises three to five times and observe how much farther back your neck can stretch. Your range of neck and back motion has likely increased.

48

ROADSIDE REST STOP

YOUR MANAGER wants that report done by the end of the day. That means overtime for certain. Your family complains that you spend too much time working late and missing dinners. Your friends think you've fallen off the planet. Forget taking care of your own personal needs. Too many people to please, and so little time. It's frustrating and feels nearly impossible to juggle all your demands and obligations. When you're sinking under a list of people to please, take a few moments to try this winding-down meditation.

1. Picture yourself on a highway. You've been in the fast lane for so long, you may have forgotten to pay attention to the warning signs to slow down. This would be an excellent time to pull over at that "Rest Area" exit up ahead.

2. Take notice of your speed and imagine shifting into a lower gear as you take the exit ramp. This is your chance to slow down everything in your mind.

3. At the rest stop, you pull into a spot with lots of trees, shade, and a balmy afternoon breeze. You can hear the hum of cars racing ahead, but that doesn't concern you now. All that really matters is just being right here, right now.

Be mindful when your energy level starts to race to the finish line, and take a few moments to pull off at the next available rest stop.

Working More
Intelligently &
Compassionately
with Others

49

EXERCISE YOUR KINDNESS MUSCLES

MOST PEOPLE know that feelings—anger, happiness, sadness, and fear, for example—are not permanent. They come and they go.

What most people don't realize is that such feelings are like muscles. They can actually be strengthened by deliberate exercise! For example, dwelling on anger and hurt actually makes those feelings stronger.

Try strengthening the feeling of kindness in your life, instead of anger.

This practice is an easy way to exercise your kindness "muscles."

1. Breathe mindfully for about a minute.

2. Set your intention. For example, "May this practice awaken greater feelings of kindness in me."

3. Think of someone you work with. Imagine speaking directly to that person in a kind voice. You

could say something like, "May you be safe and peaceful." Or, "May you be happy and healthy." Really get behind the phrase, putting all of your energy there.

4. Repeat your word or phrase gently, in your own heart, over and over, like a lullaby.

5. Try speaking to yourself with the same kindness.

FOSTER COOPERATION

A COMPETITIVE work setting encourages the individual over the group, the single person's race to the top versus a team's initiative to help everyone succeed. This can put tremendous pressure on you to perpetuate a system of inequality. Take a few minutes to infuse your work environment with a sense of cooperation and collaboration by using this mindful visualization.

1. With your eyes closed, sit in a comfortable place,

and take a moment to quiet your mind and clear your thoughts of outside distractions.

2. Picture yourself seated at a roundtable discussion with all of your managers and coworkers. You have been selected to be a part of a committee to raise consciousness around how to nurture a more team-centered atmosphere. Everyone is encouraged to brainstorm ideas on how to pool resources, share ideas, and offer assistance to each other.

3. Imagine a sense of warmth and kindness spreading across the room, touching each person in the room with a sense of camaraderie. Acknowledge the feeling of being a participant in fostering the spirit of mutual aid over cutthroat competition.

51

RITUAL FOR MUTUAL SUPPORT

IF YOU work with your spouse or partner, you may be familiar with the hazards that can arise from spending a great deal of time together. How can you maintain a more mutually cooperative connection that fosters growth and understanding? Try this one together, if possible.

1. Seated facing each other, eyes closed, knees slightly touching, observe your own breathing rhythm and movement as you sit quietly. Sense whether you have more movement in your chest or in your abdomen.

2. Say aloud or inwardly, "My intentions today are to work cooperatively and to support my partner through the complex decisions that lie ahead."

3. Open your eyes and say to each other in turn, "When we have different solutions or ideas, we will commit to finding a compromise in the hope of attaining a mutually beneficial outcome."

This practice will most certainly take time to master, but it will bring you both closer to a feeling of appreciation and support.

52

LET THE PRAISE IN

HABITUAL ENERGIES of inattention, busyness, and self-criticism can conspire to break your connection with others, including coworkers, clients, and patients.

These same habits can also diminish the personal satisfaction you get from working successfully.

This practice invites you to relax a bit and to accept praise from another for a job well done.

1. When someone begins to thank you or to praise you for a job you have done, pause and take a few mindful breaths, allowing yourself to soften and relax.

2. Turn toward the person. Make closer contact with them. Look at them, hear their voice, and listen to their words.

3. Breathe mindfully as you connect and listen.

4. Notice any reaction you have—contractions in your body, thoughts in your mind, any feelings of unease or embarrassment. Breathe and allow all of it.

5. If you wish, thank the person. Let them know you are pleased that they are satisfied and happy.

6. Later, in private if you wish, reflect on your own power to be effective and helpful, acknowledging your positive impact on others.

53

COMPASSIONATE COMMUNICATION

COMMUNICATION IS central to working with others, whether it's between you and your supervisor, coworker, customer, or client. Cultivate the good listener in yourself with this next exercise.

1. When a conversation first starts to break down or become confusing, resist the familiar temptation to get angry and frustrated. Your stress may lead to

raised voice levels or an unkind tone of voice, which rarely helps anyone feel understood.

2. Instead, try this time to consciously activate your compassionate side or the active good listener inside yourself. This starts with being patient and giving the other person fair and adequate time to speak. You may nod or ask questions, but do your best not to interrupt.

3. Observe your breathing pattern, and be mindful of each breath returning you to a state of patience and understanding.

4. Repeat back what you believe you heard the other person say, which will convey that you were listening and care about that person's opinions.

The act of compassionate listening takes practice and doesn't come easily on the first try, but the benefits will encourage a renewed feeling of camaraderie and solidarity.

54

THE MEETING WEATHER REPORT

DURING A meeting, do you ever notice that your mind is *not* where your body is?

Your body may be sending you signals that an inner storm is brewing, drawing your attention away from what's going on in the room. Inner feelings of discomfort are usually involved.

A remedy may be as simple as paying closer attention and applying some inner "self-care." Try the following practice for yourself.

1. When you notice your attention straying, bring mindfulness to your "inner weather."

2. Kindly notice and name what you're feeling— "anger," "boredom," "doubt," for example.

3. Breathe mindfully, staying with the feeling and allowing it room as you breathe.

4. Speak kindly and directly to your feeling. For example, "Thank you doubts, I feel and hear you. I get your message." Breathe mindfully, making space for your feeling with no ill will. Speak to the feeling again, kindly, if needed.

5. After some breaths practicing inner self-care, kindly return your attention to whoever is speaking.

6. Cultivate curiosity about the speaker. Practice the respect and courtesy you would like for yourself.

BETTER BOUNDARIES

THERE'S NOTHING more annoying than a coworker who takes advantage of your hospitality and can-do attitude. They're always asking for personal favors: "Will you get me something to eat while you're out?" or "Since you're leaving, can you pick me up some batteries while you're out?" And if you've kindly agreed enough times, then this situation perpetuates itself indefinitely. Since you can't change your coworker, you can only modify your behavior. This guided visualization will aid you in becoming more mindful of healthy boundaries for yourself.

1. Begin by imagining your coworker asking for yet another favor.

2. At first you may feel triggered and annoyed, so breathe into your feelings and listen to them on your inhale.

3. On your exhale, breathe out the tension and bitterness, and say aloud, "I am giving myself permission to say no. Saying no does not make me a mean person. When I say no, I am helping myself to set good boundaries for my protection."

The practice of setting proper boundaries will reduce the resentment that can build up over time toward your coworker.

56

GROW YOUR APPRECIATION OF OTHERS

WORKING WITH greater emotional intelligence includes managing your own feelings of upset and understanding the difficult behaviors of others.

Greater understanding of another's pain can help you manage any feelings of reactivity that arise when someone is rude or hurtful, allowing you to avoid taking it personally.

Increased appreciation for the other can also grow from looking more deeply at the sources of that person's pain.

1. Breathe, listen, or move mindfully for about a minute.

2. Set your intention. For example, "May this practice bring me a better relationship with my coworkers."

3. Breathe mindfully for a few more breaths.

4. Think of a difficult coworker.

5. Breathing mindfully, look deeply and see the sources of pain, the challenges, and obstacles that person may face.

6. Now see the good that person does in spite of the pain and challenges.

7. Open as deeply as possible to your own reactions, too, as you reflect.

8. Honor any guidance you receive from this practice.

57

NOTHING PERSONAL, REALLY

CRITICISM FROM your boss or supervisor is par for the course. Some of us can handle it better than others. Constructive criticism serves an important purpose in that it enables us to improve—if we listen and take heed. Useful advice can minimize accidents, increase productivity, and even save lives. Processing practical criticism requires being attentive and mindful of your old, familiar habits.

- When you receive helpful advice, do your best to first acknowledge the benefits of this new knowledge.

- Sit for a quiet moment and reflect on how those benefits might improve and expand your capacity to learn and grow.

- On your inhale, breathe in these improvements and rewards. And on your exhale, let go of your ego, your defensive side, or your hurt feelings.

Give yourself time to gradually incorporate this new protocol or information into your workday.

MAY YOUR GOOD FORTUNE NEVER END!

A BEAUTIFUL way to gladden your mind and warm your heart is to connect deeply with the joy and good fortune in another person.

For discovery and fun try the following.

1. Breathe or listen mindfully for about a minute.

2. Set your intention. For example, "May this practice bring me joy and friendship."

3. Breathe or listen mindfully for a few more breaths.

4. Focus on someone—friend or colleague—who has had good fortune—perhaps going on a vacation, having a baby, getting married, winning an award, or getting a promotion.

5. Let yourself open to their joy and well-being. Recall how happy they are, how they appear.

6. Imagine speaking to them—wishing them even more happiness. Say, for example, "May your joy and good fortune never end." Repeat your phrase silently several times.

7. Let their joy fill and comfort you.

59

DO THE BEST YOU CAN

WE'VE ALL worked with someone who, for whatever

reason, didn't carry their share of the workload. Perhaps they never mastered the fine art of multitasking, or perhaps they have a more relaxed attitude about pushing themselves seriously into the work grind. Some folks never learned to be team players. Unfortunately, if a coworker doesn't carry their load, then it can fall on your shoulders and further compound your already mountainous to-do list. The following practice will help you become more conscious of doing the best you can and not letting another's low performance tarnish your high standards.

- *The next time you're faced with this scenario, take this moment to acknowledge the difference between your coworker's expectations and your own. Ask yourself, "Is it fair to put the same expectations on everyone? Are you responsible for their performance level?"*

- *Take a few moments to inhale your feelings of frustration or resentment, and follow with exhaling and releasing your desire to change this person. Say inwardly, "Everyone works at a different pace, and they are doing the best that they can do."*

WHO'S UP, WHO'S DOWN

WHAT ARE your inner stories about those in positions "above" you or "below" you?

Does the story you tell yourself create feelings of distance or connection as you work together?

Does the story of who's "up" and who's "down" affect how you feel about yourself?

Try the following practice to better understand your stories.

1. Breathe or listen mindfully for about a minute.

2. Set your intention. For example, "May this practice give me freedom and understanding."

3. Think of someone in a position above you. Ask, "What is my story about that person?" Listen without judgment for any answer that comes.

4. Do the same for someone below you. Listen deeply without judging, defending, or arguing

with the stories.

5. Let whatever you discover guide you wisely.

61

EMOTIONAL PROTECTION

WE ALL know the difference between constructive criticism and a personal insult. But what can you do when a coworker verbally injures you? Your first reaction may be anger, disappointment, or hurt feelings. Personal insults can erode your self-confidence, if you let them, and can diminish your sense of personal achievement. Follow this ritual for protecting your feelings from others.

1. The next time a coworker or your boss is rude or says something that wounds you, take five minutes to nurture your feelings with compassion.

2. Ask yourself, "What do I need to feel validated and understood? How can I best protect my feelings from further injury and put this behind me?" You may choose to call a friend, or you might

write about it in your journal or on a notepad.

3. Compassionately consider the factors that may have led this person to react in such an emotionally abusive manner. Perhaps they have personal constraints, health challenges, or problems of their own that limit them.

Take this time to seek out the comfort and protection that you need to help you shed this negative feeling.

62

YOU DO MATTER!

DO YOU ever feel alone, isolated, ineffective, or unnecessary in your work role?

You would be very unusual if you didn't!

When you find yourself afloat in these feelings, the following practice can offer relief. Try it, even when you don't need to.

1. Breathe or listen mindfully for about a minute.

2. Set your intention. For example, "May this practice support and inspire me."

3. Breathe or listen mindfully for a few more breaths.

4. Think of someone you have helped or served today. Look deeply. See how they benefited from your service.

5. Shift your attention to a coworker or colleague. Look deeply. Notice the ways they rely on you as part of the team.

6. Breathe or listen mindfully for a few breaths more.

7. Appreciate the value you add to others' lives.

8. Let satisfaction and ease fill your heart.

63

KEEP A COOL HEAD

EVER HAD one of those dreaded days where you bark an order like a drill sergeant or you completely lose your temper with a coworker? You may feel guilty for dragging that person into your negatively charged day. When you feel like you're going to blow an emotional gasket, how can you keep your cool and not take it out on others? The following exercise will guide you to express your anger and frustration in more healing ways.

- *Take this occasion to recognize what you are feeling beneath the surface, such as disappointment, fear, resentment, or annoyance. Ask yourself, "What led me to feel this anger and irritation in the first place?"*

- *Consider what you could do to be more caring and gentle with yourself, given these circumstances. Make a brief self-care mental list, including such things as going for a walk, writing in your journal, calling your therapist, or signing up for a membership at the gym.*

Finding healthy outlets for your anger will reduce those emotional outbursts and make you feel more in control of your mood.

64

"SHIELDS UP, CAPTAIN"

IT CAN happen that a mean remark or someone's being obnoxious can leave you feeling upset or bothered.

Sometimes you can see the threat coming, as in, "Here comes so-and-so, who is always negative." Other times, meanness ambushes you.

Learning to shield yourself from meanness is one of many ways to handle it. Try the following when you need to "put up your shield."

1. When you feel or sense rudeness or meanness coming, immediately ground your attention by breathing, listening, or moving mindfully.

2. Offer yourself an affirmation. For example, "I know I am well protected."

3. Now visualize a field of protective white light instantaneously surrounding you. The light allows all necessary communication but blocks hurtful or draining energies.

4. Signal to yourself that your "light shield" is in place by saying something like, "Shields up, Captain!"

5. Let your shield down when the threat has passed.

65

BE THE KINDNESS YOU SEEK

SOME OF us have the misfortune of working in an unfriendly or even degrading work environment. You may face impolite coworkers or offensive lunchroom gossip. You may feel left out of social settings or unable to make any meaningful friendships. These kinds of disappointing work situations are enough to tarnish your normally intact optimism. You may not be able to leave your job or change the people you work alongside, so try another route. It's about attitude. Your personal attitude has the potential to reflect the pleasantries that you seek at your worksite.

1. Visualize yourself as a mirror to everyone's inherent good nature. When you smile, others might just smile back at you. When you give a compli-

ment to someone, he or she might pass one along to the next person.

2. Kindness starts from within, by taking care of your needs and then helping others. With each act of kindness, you create the possibility of igniting a wildfire of chain reactions that could have very positive results.

REAL, NOT PERFECT

MAKING DISPARAGING judgments, consciously and unconsciously, can fuel feelings of anger, uncivil behaviors, and outright meanness toward others.

If you feel critical or angry toward another, try the following practice.

1. Breathe or listen mindfully for about a minute.

2. Set your intention. For example, "May this practice bring me ease and tolerance."

3. Breathe mindfully for a few more breaths.

4. Think of someone in your workplace who annoys you. As you reflect, open to and allow all of the feelings and thoughts you have toward this person. Don't feed the feelings and don't fight the thoughts. Just notice them.

5. Ask, "What is my story about this person that causes me such pain?" Listen for the answers.

6. Ask, "Is this story really true?" Note your response.

7. Ask, "What if it isn't true? What would this person be like then?"

8. Consider the differences between being real and being perfect.

UPS AND DOWNS

STRESS OFTEN accumulates at the end of a long, laborious day. You may experience gnawing tension in your body that puts you in the worst mood. This is fertile ground for lashing out or feeling short-fused with innocent coworkers. When you experience this kind of pent-up anger in your work environment, try this stress-releasing exercise and invite your coworkers to participate.

1. From a seated position, stand up and then sit down two or three times. As you stand and sit, monitor what is happening with your toes. Do you curl your toes upward as you stand or do you point them down and grip? Studies show that people whose toes go up tend to have more neck and shoulder discomfort.

2. After having observed what happens with your toes, try this exercise two or three more times, keeping your toes and the soles of your feet in complete contact with the floor. You may have to bend a little at the hips to accomplish this task.

3. Each time you get up, practice sitting and standing while keeping your feet and toes grounded.

68

GET SILLY!

WHO LAUGHS at work? Is it possible to sprinkle fun and laughter into your daily grind? Laughter and a positive perspective can lower blood pressure, improve immune function, and reduce bodily pain. Promote your health and lighten the office atmosphere with some doses of laughter. Take this moment for really goofing off. We mean it; if you start the silliness, everyone around you will join in, and there's a good chance you'll dissipate accrued stress. Below are a few silly suggestions.

- *Do a little dance or mimic an absurd walk in front of a trusted coworker.*

- *Send out a funny joke by e-mail, if permissible.*

- *Tell someone a goofy or embarrassing story during your break.*

- *Wear a ridiculous item of clothing to work.*

Be ridiculous, get wildly creative—get silly! Laughter is infectious. Make today's goal to get others to giggle. Life has too many serious moments to wade through. Give yourself permission today to cheer up your office with some healthy chuckles.

69

A DEEPER CONVERSATION

FULL PRESENCE and attention is one of the most precious gifts you can offer another.

Mindfulness can help you be more present and attentive with friends, colleagues, and others in the workplace.

Try the following and see what happens!

1. When you are in a conversation, face to face or electronically, breathe mindfully for a few breaths as you listen. *Don't try to do any other task except listen.*

2. Include the other person more and more consciously as you steady your attention through mindful breathing.

3. If possible, look more closely at the speaker. Listen more deeply, hearing the words, the tones, and the pauses.

4. Take a mindful breath now and then as you listen, relaxing and anchoring yourself in the present moment.

5. Notice how your own inner reactions—challenging, agreeing, defending, dismissing—can distract and distance you.

6. When responding, try skillful pauses that allow your answer or statement to come from a deeper, more authentic place.

7. Enjoy any insights and sense of deeper connection you feel.

GARDEN OF GRATITUDE

How OFTEN do you make the time to openly express your gratitude toward your boss, coworkers, or clients? In our frantically driven lives, we forget to honor and give praise to the people whom we often spend more time with on a weekly basis than our own friends and families. Take just a few minutes to plant the seeds of appreciation and watch them grow. Below are a few suggestions to get you inspired.

1. Write a brief letter to a coworker telling him or her how thankful you are for all his or her hard work and commitment.

2. Let your manager or department head know how much you appreciate your job, the hours, the flexibility, or whatever pleases you about your particular situation.

3. Before you eat lunch, say grace. Express silently your appreciation for this moment of savory food, stable job, secure paycheck, and for the health and happiness of all your loved ones.

Commit to saying to every one of the employees, colleagues, or coworkers with whom you interact, "Thanks for your assistance today. I really appreciate your input and helpfulness."

71

THANK YOU VERY MUCH

IT'S EASY to criticize another for what seems to go wrong or not to work.

A totally different experience opens when you drop the criticism and see the success.

Try the following practice and enjoy a shift in perspective.

1. Breathe or listen mindfully for about a minute.

2. Set your intention. For example, "May this practice bring happiness to me and to others."

3. Breathe mindfully for a few more breaths.

4. Think of a coworker or colleague. Recall a good job they did or some success they had. Look deeply. See what they overcame. See what demands they met.

5. Breathe mindfully for a few more breaths.

6. Think again of that same person. Consider a time when they helped you. Look deeply.

7. Acknowledge their support. Thank them in any way that feels suitable.

72

BOOST YOUR STRENGTHS

WHEN YOU work for or with someone who has a condescending attitude or tone of voice, it can grind down your self-esteem and draw attention to your insecurities. You find yourself saying, "I'm too stupid. I can never get it right. What's wrong with me?" You may not be in a position to change how this patronizing person treats you, but you can alter your reaction toward these negative interactions. Bolster your self-worth by practicing this exercise.

1. The next time you feel put down, belittled, or spoken to rudely, make a list of all your duties and responsibilities, however significant or commonplace, that keep your job flowing smoothly.

2. Consider your strengths and how you utilize them daily in the work you do. Take a highlighter to your list and mark all the things you're really good at.

3. Keep this list close at hand, in your desk, briefcase, or purse, or posted on your computer. It's your daily reminder that no one can take away your talents, skills, and strong points.

73

CUT YOUR TIES

AT VARIOUS times in your life, you may have experienced profoundly emotional circumstances, such as the death of a loved one, grief, fear, crisis, and the unknown. During these psychologically draining times, you may find it very difficult to keep your personal issues at a distance in order to focus on your work. When you experience the challenges of leaving personal issues at home, practice this next letting-go exercise.

1. Sit silently with your emotions for a moment. Consider what personal feelings or memories have been stirred up during your work experience.

2. Visualize an imaginary thread that keeps you tied to the disturbing events that have surfaced today and that bind you there emotionally.

3. Picture severing these ties with a pair of scissors or a knife, freeing yourself to maintain a safe distance and giving yourself the space you need to separate from these mentally draining situations.

Travel, Deadlines, Frustrations, & Other Opportunities

74

THE ROAD TO SOLUTIONS

WHEN YOU'RE on the receiving end of other people's complaints, whether in customer service or from employee dissatisfaction or conflict, you may feel like you're being dragged down an endless, twisted path of negative feedback and unhappiness. You might feel trapped between one person's frustration and disappointment and another person's complaints about a protocol problem that's not their fault. Days like these are best handled with attentive care and kindness to everyone involved. Here's how to maintain a positive attitude as you work toward a solution.

- *As you know, lasting solutions often take time. After you've heard each side of the dilemma, take a few minutes to create a mental picture of everyone in a state of contentment. Imagine yourself on a highway of limitless possible resolutions, where each issue gets fairly addressed and everyone feels reassured.*

- *During your visualization, be open to unique and unex-*

pected signposts that may point out a different way of viewing this predicament. With new eyes, we obtain a new perspective, which can broaden our mind for discovering innovative solutions. Seeing the bigger picture allows you to become a wise vessel for receiving inventive ideas.

75

GOOD-BYE TO MR. MEAN GUY

LIKE other patterns of thinking and feeling, self-criticism and meanness become stronger with practice. Frustrations usually trigger the mean self-talk.

Most people don't realize how often or how strongly they practice self-criticism and meanness in their thoughts.

Freedom from such habits, from the inner judges constantly looking to blame, begins with mindfulness of thoughts and feelings and continues with kindness toward yourself.

1. When you feel upset, and you recognize voices of self-blame and criticism within, stop and breathe mindfully for about a minute.

2. Set your intention. For example, "May this practice free me from the habit of self-criticism."

3. Listen more closely, and imagine making space for all the negative thoughts. You don't have to fight or argue with them, and you don't have to follow them, either. Let them be. Let them go.

4. Bring mindfulness to your body. Notice any sensations of tension or holding. Breathe there. Let the space open around those sensations.

5. As you continue to breathe mindfully, gently ask, "Are those criticisms really true?" "How would I know if they were?" "How would I know if they weren't?" Listen for any answers.

LESSONS FROM NATURE

IF YOUR work demands colossal creativity to stay competitive in the market, then you probably understand feelings of stagnation when you've fallen out of the creative loop. Or perhaps you've run out of innovative and imaginative ideas for your next project. Before you throw in the towel, practice this next resourceful game, utilizing nature as your muse.

1. Building new perspectives involves removing your blinders or broadening your mind's eye in ways you've never before imagined. Let's begin by going outside and asking for help from nature. Bring your tools of the trade with you, such as camera, paintbrush, or pen.

2. From outside, select something from nature to focus your attention on—a plant, animal, insect, or snowfall.

3. Ask nature for assistance: "What can I learn from the cloud bank?" or "What do bees know about my project?" or "What advice would my dog offer about my dilemma?"

4. Be patient and receptive to the whispers of wisdom and untold secrets from places that you never dreamed of. Let nature's limitless splendor and beauty guide you.

77

WATCH YOUR BACK

FRUSTRATION and stress, a demanding sense of urgency, or just feeling overloaded can lead to inattention and poor body mechanics during physical activities at work or during breaks. Your back often pays the price for untended stress and distraction.

Learn to protect your back by tuning in to it more mindfully and more often.

Try the following practice to increase mindfulness of your back.

1. Breathe mindfully for about a minute.

2. Set your intention. For example, "May I protect my back through greater awareness."

3. Bring attention to your back. Let in the sensations of the low back, mid-back, and upper back and shoulders, kindly and without judgment.

4. Acknowledge tightness or stiffness. Imagine that

as you breathe, the out-breath carries away unnecessary tension or stress.

5. Your back is your friend. Say thank you to it now and then, and pay mindful attention whenever you use it.

ASKING YOUR HIGHER POWER

Do you feel underpaid and undervalued at your current employment? You put in your time, you've been reliable, dependable, and committed, and yet you're still not gaining your fair share financially. Perhaps the company is downsizing, or they've just announced that there's been a freeze on all pay raises and promotions. What can you do?

- *Start by considering your options carefully and conspiring with the universe to get what you really want and need from your life.*

- *Make a mental list of the best possible scenarios, such as a pay hike, promotion, or perfect job opportunity presenting itself.*

- *Ask yourself: What would it take for you to feel appreciated and valued for the work that you do?*

- *Share this knowledge with your friends and family. Consider including it when you give thanks at a meal.*

- *Perform a brief, personal ceremony in your mind where you hand off this sacred request to your higher power. Be aware of powerful possibilities infiltrating your life in unexpected ways.*

79

EMERGENCY MANAGEMENT

ON THE job (or anytime), when you feel suddenly overwhelmed by any distressing feeling—pain, fear, doubt, anger, frustration, for example—try the following for "emergency management."

1. Immediately bring mindful attention, informed by kindness and self-compassion, directly to your inner life.

2. Open and allow the sensations in your body and

the activity of any thoughts you are having. Notice the "tone of voice" of those thoughts.

3. If you can, name the feeling: "anger" or "fear," for example.

4. Breathe mindfully for a few breaths more while you include—don't fight—the upset. Continue to kindly name the experience that is happening. Meet it without ill will.

5. As you breathe mindfully, imagine that a vast space begins to open within you and surrounds all of the sensations and thoughts, allowing them to come and go more freely.

6. Have patience and faith in yourself as you breathe mindfully and rest more and more in this space. What do you discover?

80

OUT OF HARM'S WAY

WHEN YOUR work shift puts you under dire stress, you need immediate focus and concentration. Under this kind of critical pressure, there's no room for carelessness or mistakes to be made. Start each workday with a relaxation practice in order to ground yourself in the present and center yourself throughout your day.

- *Be aware of the tempo of your breathing, and take note of whatever feelings or sensations you may be experiencing in this moment. Are you rested and alert, or are you anxious? Are you irritated by a previous event? Are you feeling joy, apathy, or depression?*

- *From a standing position, feet firmly grounded on the floor, take three easy breaths, and on each inhale say to yourself, "I am conscious of my mood and thoughts." "I am aware of my connection to this earth." "I am in my body right now."*

- *On each exhale speak your intentions: "May this moment ground me to the present, bring me a sense of tranquillity, and keep me out of harm's way."*

When you are constantly under severe work demands that put you in potentially dangerous circumstances, start out your shift with a mindful practice of reaffirming your ability to center yourself in the here and now.

81

GO AHEAD, PLEASE

NEVER underestimate the power of generosity. It can bring ease and joy into otherwise rushed or tense moments and situations.

While traveling (or anytime), explore the power of mindfulness coupled with generosity.

1. Learn to recognize that sense of inner rushing, irritation, or upset in yourself.

2. Acknowledge the upset with kindness and compassion for yourself. Gently remind yourself that feeling upset is *not* a failure or a defect.

3. Breathe or listen mindfully for about a minute.

4. Set your intention. For example, "May I discover more about stress and the power of generosity."

5. Look around for opportunities to help someone, and do it! For example, let someone go ahead of you in line, give up your parking space, offer someone your seat, offer to help someone in need.

6. Without expectation or judgment, notice how you feel after each gift.

82

SELF-PRESERVATION FIRST

YOUR WORK may demand a lot of you. Your high level of responsibility may force you to be under the gun for time and pressured to drop whatever you're doing. This can put your mind and body into a tailspin of stress and anxiety. You may have skipped a meal or forgotten to meet your basic needs before you rushed off to work. Self-care doesn't come easily for most people, but it is a necessary part of restoring a sense of well-being and good health. Take a few minutes to unwind from this frantic momentum with the intention of self-preservation.

- Begin by making a mental list of your basic human needs for each and every day of your life, such as water, shelter, food, warmth, clothes, and so on.

- Take note of the things that you ignored while you scurried *to meet work demands. Did you forget to drink water today? When was your last sit-down meal? Did you skip the gym?*

- *What can you do in this moment that would enable you to take better care of yourself? For example, keep your body hydrated, order food to be delivered, or wash your hands and face to cool your frayed nerves.*

In the future, consider keeping a water bottle with you at all times or packing some snacks before you leave for work.

83

JUST FOR YOU

WHENEVER YOU feel overburdened or overly busy, traveling or anywhere, take five good minutes just for yourself.

This is a time to put down the busyness and step out of the momentum of doing. A time to find the freedom that lies in stopping and letting things be.

1. Breathe or listen mindfully for about a minute.

2. Set your intention. For example, "May this practice give me peace and ease."

3. Continue breathing or listening mindfully.

4. For the rest of this meditation, allow yourself to let go of any planning, explaining, or defending.

5. No need to fight or argue, even with annoying thoughts or other distractions.

6. Let the meditation—attention on breath or sounds—carry you. Go as deeply as feels safe.

7. Feel and appreciate the life flowing through you in this moment.

84

RED ALERT!

THE MAIN computer server at work is down, everyone's in a panic, and you're the one in charge. Or crisis breaks out at an off-site job in another state, and you've been called in to fix it. When fast-paced problem solving is paramount under a tight deadline, it's critical to keep yourself from reeling out of control with panic and distress. Critical and technical decisions need to be made with a cool head. The following exercise is a guide for boosting your patience and endurance while under extreme pressure.

- *Start by focusing on your breathing rhythm and movement while you're sitting or working on-site. Are you holding your breath, or breathing naturally? Is there more movement in your chest, or your abdomen? Breathing rapidly from the chest can lead to bodily tension and fatigue.*

- *Practice slowing your breathing rate and lowering the location of the movement of your breath to your abdomen.*

- *Set your intentions by saying, "Despite this work crisis, I am restoring patience and stamina with each breath."*

Give yourself permission to move carefully and methodically through each task, which will improve your ability to work under duress.

85

FEELING TIRED?

EFFECTIVE self-care arises from self-awareness joined with kindness and compassion.

A good time to practice self-care is anytime you are feeling tired, and especially if you are feeling exhausted.

Instead of feeding anger, negative self-talk, or feelings of despair over being tired, try the following practice.

1. Breathe or listen mindfully for about a minute.

2. Set your intention. For example, "May this practice bring me ease."

3. Focus mindful attention on your "inner body"—sensations, energy level, degree of alertness.

4. Compassionately acknowledge any feelings of fatigue or dullness. There's no need to fight, avoid, or defend them. Simply breathe mindfully, allowing and including the feelings in your awareness in this moment.

5. Gently ask, "How can I best care for myself at this time?" Listen for all the answers.

6. With kindness and compassion, choose your wisest response.

86

SAFETY BUBBLE

THERE ARE times in your life when you may feel riddled with fears—the fear of displeasing your supervisor, the fear of failing to meet a deadline, or the fear of the wrath of an angry boss. These bottled-up anxieties can trigger enormous stress and make you feel unsafe and insecure in your workplace. This next visualization may be useful for creating a place of emotional safety and security.

1. Begin by finding a quiet place at your cubicle or work site and closing your eyes. Free your mind of nagging worries and give yourself permission to just rest peacefully for a few moments.

2. Draw an imaginary protective bubble or fence

around your immediate circumference. Say aloud or to yourself, "I am protected from my inner fears and worries within this circle of safety. No harm can come to me here."

3. Now gradually extend your protective barrier outward to include the room that you're in or your surrounding environment. Visualize your expansive safety net to further encompass more and more things, such as people, pets, loved ones, coworkers, and even the planet.

Remember to return to this mental shelter for security when you feel threatened or unsafe.

87

YOUR SPACES IN THE 24/7

Do you find that your work requires a time commitment of twenty-four hours and seven days a week, at least at times?

During such periods of intensity, your work and your life are one.

Self-care in such demanding times is vital and especially potent. You can find compassionate care living in the spaces inside your 24/7 routine.

1. Intentionally look for spaces—moments to pause—scattered throughout your 24/7 commitment.

2. Pick any space, and breathe or listen mindfully for the entire time. How does that feel?

3. Pick another space. Do a deep-relaxation practice or an inspiring, energizing one.

4. Pick another space. Take strength from the "Big Picture"—the greater meaning your job holds.

5. Pick another space. Ask, "What are my supports in this moment?"

6. Let all the spaces sustain you.

88

REKINDLE THE JOY

AT VARIOUS moments in your life, you may feel less connected to the work that you do. Your daily routine loses its spark, and you come up empty for inspiration. Each day launches you on a treacherous uphill battle that leaves you drained and discouraged by the end of the shift. What can you do to rekindle meaning and joy in the workplace?

1. First, think back on the times when you felt moments of pleasure and invested curiosity in your tasks. Did you just master a new software program? Was it after the announcement of a promotion? Did you enjoy training others and discovering their skills?

2. While you recall those times of feeling connected and fulfilled by engaging work, exhale very quietly with a slight smile.

3. Consider ways that you can incorporate those once joyful or meaningful tasks into your current

routine. If you dislike working alone, can you find tasks that involve team dynamics? If you hate your routine, can you inquire about exploring new areas for furthering your skills?

This is your opportunity to stop complaining about what's wrong and to engage and commit to challenging yourself in new ways.

89

I DID WHAT!?!

EVERYONE HAS had the experience of being their own worst critic.

Modern behavioral medicine recognizes this, and research shows that what you think and how you talk to yourself about it can have an impact—positive or negative—on your health.

When the "judges are in session" in your mind, being critical over anything, try the following.

1. Breathe or listen mindfully for about a minute.

2. Set your intention. For example, "May this practice give me peace."

3. Breathe mindfully for a few more breaths.

4. Focus attention on any negative or critical thoughts you're having. Let them speak without defending yourself or arguing with them.

5. Breathe mindfully. Remind yourself that you are *not* your thoughts. Ask, "Are these thoughts true?" Ask, "How would I know it?"

6. Listen for any answers with kindness and compassion for yourself.

YOUR TRUE INNER VOICE

IT'S NOT always an easy decision to take that newly offered career opportunity or promotion. In fact, it can destabilize you emotionally. You may feel trapped between the loyalty you feel for your current employer and your desire for advancement. This is a difficult position to be in and requires paying attention to your own inner voice of wisdom. This next exercise is a guide to listening to your true inner calling and staying on your path of self-discovery.

- *Start with a simplified list of the pros and cons of your current job versus the new job offering. Weigh factors like your relationships, friendships, location, stress level, and so on.*

- *Without making a final decision, sit with the emotions that you are experiencing right now. Are you scared of the unknown? Are you concerned about disappointing people? Are you fearful of making an irreversible decision?*

- *Remember to be conscious of your breathing pattern, letting in reassuring thoughts on your inhalation while letting go of troublesome thoughts on your exhalation. In this brief silent moment, be open and receptive to your voice of reason and trust in your ability to figure out what's best for you.*

91

TRAVEL SMART

TRAVELING, ESPECIALLY in these times, can be very stressful!

Packing some emotional intelligence can be a big help in easing the stress. Include self-awareness, self-care, and wise management of your reactions when you pack.

1. In the airport, on a train or bus, in a security line, crowded on a plane—wherever you are—anchor and steady your attention with mindful breathing or listening.

2. Affirm yourself. For example, "I can manage successfully. I have all the intelligence, courage, strength, and support I need."

3. Bring mindfulness to your inner life. If you feel hurried, visualize stress floating away with each out-breath. If you feel anxious, imagine that each in-breath fills you with peace and ease. If you feel

angry or annoyed, silently wish those around you safety and well-being.

4. May all your travels be safe and protected.

92

SHOUT IT OUT

WE'VE ALL been given bad directions or gotten stuck in horrific traffic. And not all of us have the luxury of a software program installed into our car consoles or Palm Pilots with driving directions translated into thirty-two languages. You're lost, driving in circles, and you're late for an important business meeting or appointment. It's enough to skyrocket your stress levels into road rage. Ask yourself this: what's another five minutes when you're already late? If you're about to meet a high-profile client, why not take a few minutes to liberate your fury and let off some mental steam, preferably when you're alone.

- *Take one deep breath and on the exhale, with your mouth open wide, holler or shout one or two exclama-*

tions, such as "Ahhh!" or "Yes! Yes! Yes!" or "I can do this!" Give it a few tries and really belt it out.

- How do you feel? Were you embarrassed or self-conscious if anyone could hear or see you? Did it feel like a release of some pent-up frustration?

- Fill your lungs with air again and shout out something new, such as "I feel alive!" or "I'm on top of the world!" or "I'm a force of nature!" Feel free to holler out your joys, sorrows, or frustrations.

- Observe your heartbeat, the rhythm of your breathing, and any other bodily sensations. What changes do you notice?

93

FEELING CROWDED?

DOES IT seem when you're traveling that the seats have all shrunk and that there are more and bigger people in them?

When you are feeling crowded, even after doing everything possible to maximize your physical space, use the following practice to rest in limitless *inner* space.

1. Close your eyes and breathe or listen mindfully for about a minute.

2. Set your intention. For example, "May this practice release me into ease and peace."

3. Bring gentle attention to your body. Imagine that as you breathe out, tension and stress float away with each breath. Feel your body relax and grow heavier.

4. Shift your focus to sounds. Listen mindfully. Find the space between the sounds, noticing how each arises and returns from that silent space. Let your mind and heart rest there.

5. As often as you like, when you feel steady and more relaxed, wish yourself well using a phrase like, "May I be safe and filled with peace."

94

BEAT THE FATIGUE

IF YOUR job requires long work hours, you may be all too familiar with job fatigue. Your eyes feel heavy, your body gets groggy, and it's all you can do not to fall asleep. You might wait for the moment to pass, but eventually the exhaustion catches up with you. This next exercise is to help you stay more alert and improve your concentration.

- *Take note of your posture and body position. Are you slouching, shoulders rolled forward, neck stiff?*

- *Consider making a few adjustments that will improve your comfort and allow you to feel more at ease in your body. You may want to open the window for a gust of fresh air or guzzle down some water for replenishment.*

- *Steer your mind away from thoughts of the long road ahead of you and focus on where you are at this given moment. What new observations can you uncover on your journey today?*

Pay attention to your surroundings. You might just discover new and untapped beauty that you never noticed before. Let it revive you.

95

NOT ANOTHER DEADLINE!

SOONER OR later everyone hits that wall where they feel completely stressed out.

The straw that breaks the camel's back can be something as routine as one more deadline, one more meeting, or one more thing to do.

For immediate relief, try the following.

1. Push back from your desk or step back from your workstation and find some privacy.

2. Breathe or listen mindfully for about a minute.

3. Set your intention. For example, "May this practice bring me relief and ease."

4. Breathe or listen mindfully for a few more breaths.

5. Think of one thing you are grateful for. Name it. Be concrete—for example, "I am healthy enough to work. I have friends and family who love me."

6. Relax, breathe mindfully, and ask, "What are some other blessings in my life?" Listen for any response and acknowledge that.

7. Offer an affirmation. For example, "I remember that I have all the support I need."

8. Continue wise self-care as you work.

96

SHAKE OUT THOSE WORRIES

Do you suffer with the worry bug? The carousel of bothersome uncertainties is endless, especially if your work involves travel: "What if I miss my flight? Maybe I'm at the wrong airport or aboard the wrong plane? What if my luggage doesn't make it to my connecting flight in time?" Chronic worries can leave you feeling anxious and fretful over every conceivable negative scenario. You may experience high blood pressure, rapid heartbeat, unsettled stomach, and clenching of the muscles in your jaw, neck, and back. It's time for a distraction to set free all those nagging concerns about things that you're likely powerless to control.

1. Focus on your breath, reminding yourself that each breath is your personal and miraculous link to restoring calm and peace. You may not be able to control the arrival of your flight, but you can breathe in a more relaxed state of being and breathe out your anxieties.

2. Observe how you feel in your body, carefully adjusting your body to a more comfortable and at-ease position. Be mindful of areas where you store your tension, and breathe oxygen into those areas.

3. Now shake out your body, jiggle your hands and arms, wiggle your torso, flex your legs and feet. Don't be shy. Shake off those worries the way a dog shakes off water from its body.

97

HATE THAT NOISE?

WORK CONDITIONS can be pretty noisy sometimes.

Do you ever find yourself in an inner war against the noise and distractions?

They don't all have to be quiet or go away for you to find relief. Try the following practice to explore the peace that lies within you.

1. In the midst of the noise, sit back and breathe or listen mindfully for about a minute.

2. Offer yourself an affirmation. For example, "I have what I need to cope with noise."

3. Check your "inner weather" with kindness and compassion. Acknowledge and respect any feelings of frustration or ill will you sense. Breathe mindfully, not fighting these feelings and not feeding them. Let them come and go.

4. Turn your attention back toward the sounds. Listen mindfully to all sounds, including the

annoying ones. Drop the fight. Name the aversion you feel. Notice the story in your mind. Relax. Let it all be as you listen mindfully. Notice how sounds change and how space and peace can grow in you.

5. Let the peace support you as you resume your work.

98

CLOSE AT HEART

SOME OF you might travel often for business trips or attend meetings that require being out of town for extended periods. Time away from your home, family, and friends can leave you feeling homesick and heavyhearted. You may have missed your child's recital or first game of the season. You may miss your sweetie or your best friend's birthday get-together. Being away can take its toll on your sense of connectedness and emotional support. The following exercise will open your heart's doorway for love and rekindle your feelings of personal connection.

1. In your heart there is a complex map of inter-woven, artery-like highways that lead to each and every person who has ever loved you and whom you love too, since the day you were born.

2. Visualize this elaborate roadway, all the dips and turns, signs and symbols, bridges and streams, caverns and mountains, valleys and lakes.

3. Consider where each thread leads: grandparents, sister-in-law, grandchild, childhood friend, first boyfriend or girlfriend, and your favorite babysitter.

Remember that each of these threads will steer you in the direction of a love that can never be too far from your heart, or forgotten.

99

THAT OBNOXIOUS PERSON AND YOU

HERE THEY come again! You know who—that obnoxious one. That person is not fun, not agreeable, and definitely not pleasant.

The interaction leaves you filled with ill will, distress, even outrage.

But remember, you can protect yourself and set the upset down.

1. During the interaction, use mindful breathing to anchor and support yourself.

2. At times, offer a silent affirmation. For example, "I am wise and strong enough to handle this situation."

3. As you listen to that person's words, see how they are trying to be happy, too, just like everyone else.

4. As you look at that person, imagine him or her as a child. What pain did they suffer?

5. When you speak, try wishing that person happi-

ness. For example, "I'm sorry to hear that. I hope things get better."

6. Protect yourself. Mindfully set limits and disengage respectfully.

7. As you leave that person, turn your attention and open heart to your next breath.

100

AIRPORT BODY RELIEF

IF YOUR job requires frequent travel, you've spent a lot of time in airports. You've had your fair share of delayed flights, which resulted in missed connections, leaving you feeling drained and taxed before you even got started.

There are worse places on the planet to get stuck than an airport, but this is no consolation when you're feeling trapped and fatigued, and there are people who are waiting for you at your destination. Take a few minutes between flights, despite the lack of privacy, to do some much-needed arm and shoulder stretches.

- *From a standing position, preferably in flat shoes or shoeless, place your feet shoulder-width apart.*

- *Breathe mindfully for one or two breaths. Stay conscious of air filling your lungs and air leaving your lungs.*

- *Weave your fingers together and stretch them toward the ceiling with your palms facing upward. Hold for thirty seconds.*

- *Relax your arms at your sides and then repeat this exercise three to five times.*

Notes

Notes